Gay USA ™

FIRST BOOKS

P.O. Box 578147
Chicago, IL 60657
312-276-5911

ACKNOWLEDGMENTS

A book like this can only be written with the help of many people. I met hundreds of folks along the way. I would especially like to thank Jeremy Solomon of First Books and Sara London, my editor. For their help, advice, and insights, special thanks to Sid Wilson and Steve Smith, who were exemplary tour guides. Other helpful sources, hosts, advisors, and guides were Deacon Maccubbin, Jack Pelham, Ed Hermance, Jim Hooten, Cliff Bostock, Adolf Douttel, Carrie Barnette, Brett Shingledecker, Paul West, Brian Gately, Bill Stuart, Eldon Johnson, Eric Maltman, George Chilson, Frank Rose, Michael Ingram, Keith Robinson, Michael McVay, Mark McGrew, Betty Pearl, John Shore, Hugo Castro, Lisa Price, Ron Kraft, Allen Amberg, Michael Aller, and Fran Golden.

Author: George Hobica
Publisher and Editor: Jeremy Solomon
Editorial Consultant: Sara London
Design/Production: Miles & Gale DeCoster, Art Machine, Inc.

ISBN 0-912301-29-5

Manufactured in the United States of America.

Published by First Books, Inc., P.O. Box 578147, Chicago, IL 60657, 312-276-5911.

C O N T E N T S

3

Dedicated to the memory of my father, to my mother, and to Allen.

Gay USA is the first book of its kind: a selective, impartial, but opinionated travel guide to the United States for gay travelers, and one without any advertising of any kind. I personally conducted all the research in this book, traveling around the country to do so. I ate the meals, slept in the guest houses, worked out in the gyms, and ogled the strippers in the bars myself—*somebody* had to do it.

Writing a gay guide book isn't all fun and games, though. I wore out a lot of sneaker rubber, slept in a lot of uncomfortable beds (most of which I've exorcised from my memory and this book), and ate a lot of bad meals. But I also met a huge number of helpful, kind people and learned a lot about what this country's major cities and gay resorts have to offer.

You'll notice that not every city in the country is covered in this guide. I preferred to keep the book small, focusing on the largest and most popular gay destinations. I've made every attempt to update the information. Having said that, please realize that it's in the very nature of gay travel and entertainment to always be on the cutting edge. So things will change, and although all effort has been made to assure accuracy, we cannot guarantee it. So please call ahead.

There was a great temptation, as a professional travel writer, to include non-gay restaurants and hotels, especially when a good gay alternative didn't exist. I've tried to resist that lure. This is a gay guide book, and although I briefly mention a few mainstream hotels and restaurants in the Cities section, I do so just as a quick reference. I recommend you obtain an *Access* or *Birnbaum* guide to learn more about mainstream services and attractions. I also tried to distinguish between truly gay restaurants and lodgings and merely gay-friendly or even gay-owned ones. There is a difference, and while there's nothing wrong with gay-friendly or gay-owned, when *I* travel I like to know the difference.

In writing this book, too, I've made some basic assumptions about you readers. First, that you're fairly cultured, that you like historic homes and museums more than professional wrestling, so that's what I've concentrated on in the "See/do" section. I also assume you like to keep fit when you travel, so I've included gay gyms, if they exist, in each city. Chances are if I've left a guest house, restaurant, or club out, it's because I felt it wasn't a good experience, or I wasn't convinced it was going to be in existence by the time this book appeared.

What I hope I've written is a concise, honest, and accurate assessment of the places most visited by gay travelers in the US. I hope you enjoy using Gay USA and that I bump into you along the way!

—George Hobica

Gay USA

THE CITIES

ATLANTA

AREA CODE 404

WHAT TO EXPECT

A tlanta, known to party-circuit animals for the tribal event called Hotlanta, is more complex than it seems at first. In fact, it's a bit schizoid—both liberal and conservative at once. First, the liberal side. People feel free to hold hands and show affection on the streets. You see a lot of rainbow flags hanging in store windows and stuck to car bumpers. Even a straight-owned brake shop with many gay clients flies the colors. And people don't put the brakes on in the bars and clubs; unlike in some other cities, strippers take it all off in Atlanta, and some bars are allowed to stay open 24 hours a day.

On the other hand, outside the Interstate 285 perimeter the city is surrounded by Bible-thumping rednecks. Witness the unfortunate politics of nearby Cobb County, which adopted a resolution in 1993 condemning the gay lifestyle. And you can't rent X-rated videos, gay or straight, anywhere in Atlanta. Even some gay groups are politically cautious. The local Queer Nation chapter, before it disbanded, debated changing "Queer" to something less in-your-face. "People believe they'll get civil rights passively," says Cliff Bostock, a local writer, "by sanitizing pride parades, by making gays more palatable." The South was held together for years with manners, he points out, and there's still a premium on being nice at all costs. Asked whether Atlanta was a gay-affirming city, another local gay newspaper writer hesitated a moment and replied, "Well, it's not as homophobic as most." A *Southern Voice* survey found that 50% of respondents described themselves as totally or partially closeted.

The estimated 300,000 gays and lesbians who live in the metro area, escapees from hundreds of small Southern towns, are scattered about rather than ghettoized. But they're also integrated into the mainstream of Atlanta life, which helps explain why there's no true gay central. Many gays and lesbians have moved to outlying districts. Just ask the Diggin' Dykes of Decatur, a suburban women's garden club. One result of the sprawl and laissez-faire zoning is that the most adorable "Leave it to Beaver" neighborhoods are just a 90-second walk from tawdry strips with sleazy bars. A closeted Ward Cleaver could step out for a quart of milk and stop by his favorite fetish club on the way, with no one the wiser.

You'll spend a lot of time in your car here. Like Dallas, Atlanta sprawls. But unlike Dallas, which has a definable gay epicenter, Atlanta is more amorphous. The Ansley Mall/Ansley Square complex is the closest thing to a nerve center; that or the Midtown area, home to several gay-friendly restaurants, gay clubs, and a gay-oriented guest house. Midtown has had its ups and downs, though—and at night it's not all that genteel. On Cypress Street, outside a semi-seedy bar called Metro, I encountered a lithe, shirtless, hollow-eyed young hustler scribbling a poem ("Cypress Treat," he called it) on an alley wall: "People say I live on this street/But I know that's not true/The truth is I die on this street/Because that is what I choose to do."

BEST TIME TO COME

Any time but summer, although the Hotlanta extravaganza is held in Aug.

10

GETTING AROUND

You'll need a car, but the MARTA rapid transit system is very efficient.

STAY

GAY

Hidden Creek (201 N. Mill Rd, 705-9545). About 15 min from downtown in a quiet suburban area, the name of this former private home makes it sound like a summer camp; but it's a tastefully-appointed, modern, 5,000 sq ft house that caters exclusively to gay men. Tries to maintain a low sexual temperature. The seven rooms feature interesting furnishings and most offer private baths. Over two acres of secluded land. Cocktail hour with free set-ups and snacks, nude sunbathing, Jacuzzi, inviting common rooms. Scott and Tom are the amiable hosts. Rates: $65-$75 single, $85-$95 double, $20 for extra person in room.

GAY-FRIENDLY

Midtown Manor (811 Piedmont Ave, NE, 872-5846). Not gay-owned, but 75% gay clientele (markets heavily to gay travelers, hoping to become 100% gay). In a convenient area for gay attractions, but only so-so rooms (hand-me-down furnishings, not-new shag carpeting, suspended ceilings—you know the look). Sixty rooms in two buildings. No private baths. Full or double beds, direct dial phones with individual phone number for each room. Off-street parking. Rates: $45-$85.

BEST BEDS

The two **Ritz Carltons** are the best hotels in town. Usual flawless service, especially on the bow and scrape concierge floors where you'll find heavenly oatmeal cookies and free drinks. Of the two—Buckhead (3434 Peachtree Rd, NE, 237-2700) and Downtown (181 Peachtree St, NE, 659-0400)—the former is marginally better.

SEE/DO

TEN THINGS NO SELF-RESPECTING GAY PERSON SHOULD MISS

Fox Theatre (660 Peachtree St). Tour this lavishly restored 1929 Moorish/Egyptian/Deco fantasy; tours are given at 10 am through the Atlanta Preservation Center (876-2041).

11

World of Coca Cola Pavilion (55 M. L. King Jr Blvd, 676-5151). Self-guided tours begin every half hour—call ahead for reservations during summer.

Underground Atlanta (Alabama and Peachtree Sts, 523-2311). Popular shopping, dining and entertainment complex.

The CNN Center tour (Marietta at Techwood Dr, 827-2491). Inside look at the fourth network's world headquarters.

The High Museum of Art (1280 Peachtree St, 892-HIGH). Atlanta's best collection of European and American paintings, 20th-century art, and African paintings.

Hotlanta (874-3976). Annual gay party each Aug with male beauty pageant and rafting down the Chattahoochi River.

Little Five Point area (near the junction of Euclid and Moreland Aves). Tour Atlanta's SoHo.

Stone Mountain State Park (US 78, 498-5690). Hike through this large memorial to Confederate heroes, ante-bellum plantation, museums.

Guy's and Doll's (2788 E. Ponce de Leon Ave, 377-2956). Attend a show at this Chippendales rip-off catering to gays as well as straight women.

Piedmont Park. Rent a bike or rollerblades (from Skate Escape, 1086 Piedmont Ave, 892-1292) and glide through the city's main green space.

KEEP FIT/RECREATION

Boot Camp (1544 Piedmont Ave, Ansley Mall, 876-8686). All-gay gym, mostly free weights. Day fee: $10.

Fitness Factory (500 Amsterdam Ave, Midtown Outlet, 815-7900). Gay-owned and -operated, in a conveniently-located strip mall, the newest gay gym in town with 7,000 sq ft of hot, sweaty men and machines. Day fee: $10.

Mid-City Fitness Center (2201 Faulkner Rd, 321-6507). Almost all gay, the best of the bunch. Biggest, cleanest, best looking men. Aerobics, ab classes, tanning, good mix of machines and weights, 15,000 sq ft Day fee: $12.

EAT

TRES GAY

Flying Biscuit (1655 McLendon Ave at Clifton, 687-8888). Tasty home cooking in a funky storefront atmosphere, lesbian-run, lots of gay/lesbian clientele. Breakfast served all day. Favorite dish: Love Cakes (black bean and cornmeal cakes topped with tomatillo salsa). Entrees: breakfast and lunch under $8, dinner items $12-$13.

Our Friend's Place (1491 Piedmont Ave, Ansley Sq, 875-8980). Restaurant in a bar called Spectrum. Basic food. Entrees: $4-$14

GAY FRIENDLY

Einstein's (1077 Juniper, 876-7925). *Out* magazine listed this Midtown eatery as one of the gayest restaurants in the US. Not! It depends on when you go; it could just as easily be ladies who lunch and business types. On my visit, I counted about 30% gay. Sun brunch is said to be the gayest meal. Pleasant patio out front, lots of rabbit-warren small rooms inside, decent and varied menu. Entrees: $10-$17.

Partners (1399 N. Highland Ave, 876-8104). Loud, wildly popular, no-reservations eatery with almost all-gay staff but largely straight clientele. Offerings might include Delaware crabcakes and Tuscan duck. Entrees: $15-$18.

Vickery's (1106 Crescent Ave, 881-1106). Voted best patio dining in Atlanta, this is a more upscale restaurant than nearby Einstein's. Probably 50% gay clientele. Owners support gay causes, and most of the waiters are gay–and cute. A special of herb roasted chicken with port-smoked mushroom sauce is typical of the fare. Entrees: $7-$16.

Virginia's Koffie House (1243 Virginia Ave, 875-4453). Gay-owned coffee house with salads and other light fare. Many gay clients, Gen X types. Entrees: under $7.

TOP TABLES

Dining Room at the Ritz Carlton Buckhead (3434 Peachtree Rd, 237-2700, prix fixe $56) is the best restaurant in Atlanta. Formal (coat and tie), but not outrageously expensive considering what you get.

PLAY/MEET

MOSTLY FOR DANCING

The Armory (836 Juniper St, 881-9280). Part of the so-called "homo-plex" in the Midtown area, this is the smaller of Atlanta's two main dance arenas. People come here first, and then move on to Backstreet (see below) across the parking lot. Single sound system plays throughout.

Backstreet (845 Peachtree St, 873-1986). This 24-hour club, which doesn't really get started until late, is Atlanta's biggest all-gay dance venue with four levels of good-looking guys. Catch the x-rated Charlie Brown's Cabaret at 11:30 pm Fri and Sat. Gift shop.

Revolution (293 Pharr Rd, 816-5455). This club in a former car dealership showroom is convenient if you're staying in Buckhead. Sun tea dance at 7 pm.

MOSTLY FOR CRUISING/DRINKING

Blake's (845 Peachtree, 873-1986). Midtown bar within walking distance of Backstreet, popular with young stand-and-model types. Nice outdoor space overlooking parking lot.

Burkhardt's (Ansley Sq Mall, 872-4403). Arguably the friendliest place, with some of the best-looking men, in town. Free buffet Sun 4-8 pm.

Metro (6th and Cypress, 874-9869). Don't bring mom. Here, wasted twenty-something male prostitutes mingle with Generation-X types indulging in midday beer and joints.

Velvet (89 Park Pl, 681-9936). Currently Mon (10 pm-2 am) and Sat (11 pm-2 am) are the gay nights at this attractive club where gym boys and club kids meet.

AFRICAN-AMERICAN

Loretta's (708 Spring St, 874-8125). Happening African-American bar on two floors with great music.

FOR LESBIANS

The Otherside (1924 Piedmont Rd, 875-5238). In Buckhead, essentially a women's bar trying to attract more men.

14 LEATHER BARS

The Eagle (308 Ponce de Leon Ave, 873-2453). One of the best DJ's in town, no real dress code.

The Heretic (2069 Cheshire Bridge Rd, 325-3061). Near a suburban-like neighborhood, but trying to be the naughtiest place in town. "Backroom" for groping, which requires leather or no shirt for admission.

SHOP

In addition to world-class malls, Atlanta has tons of gay-owned shopping, with the Ansley Mall area a particular focus. Here's a sampling:

Bill Halman Boutique (1054 N. Highland Ave, 876-6055). This fashion forward boutique in the Virginia Highlands features the upmarket creations of its gay owner.

Brushstrokes (1510 Piedmont Ave, 876-6567). Ansley Sq purveyor of gay magazines, cards, T-shirts, posters, etc.

Heavy Duty Design (656 N. Highland Ave, 873-0036). Gay-owned emporium full of witty, durable tableware and kitchen stuff.

Malepak (2000 Cheshire Bridge Rd, 321-0603) Gym, swim, and club-wear. Teeny-weenie posing trunks, striped and sequined bikinis. Catalog.

Poster Hut (2175 Cheshire Bridge Rd, 633-7491). Adult gift shop with prints, sculptures, cards, leather, club clothes.

RESOURCES

GENERAL INFORMATION

Atlanta Convention & Visitors Bureau info center (Peachtree Center Mall, 233 Peachtree St, NE, Suite 2000, Atlanta 30303, 521-6600).

Newcomer's Handbook™ **for Atlanta** (First Books, 312-276-5911). Tremendously useful book for anyone (gay or straight) *moving* here.

GAY/HIV INFORMATION

Atlanta Gay Center (67 12th St, 876-5372). A good place to get information, although this group doesn't represent mainstream opinion in gay Atlanta and isn't terribly popular.

15

BOOKSTORE

Outwrite (Midtown Promenade, 931 Monroe, 607-0082). You can get a cup of coffee and a snack here and sit among the books.

PUBLICATIONS

Southern Voice (876-1819). Larger, more serious tabloid paper.

ETC (525-3821). Small-format magazine.

BOSTON

AREA CODE 617

WHAT TO EXPECT

Barely 20 years ago, Boston was a backwater. Sure, proper Bostonians still called it "The Hub of the Universe" and the "Athens of America." But the summer I drove a big yellow Caprice for the Checker Taxi Company (I still have the shiny-visored cap) the now-fashionable homes in the western edge of the Back Bay were, if not exactly slums, then certainly not genteel. The vestibules stank from a combination of Lestoil and stale urine (this was in the days when a cab driver would actually go in and *ring the doorbell* instead of honking his horn) and the mailboxes had all been broken into, even as far east as Dartmouth Street. Today, those same brownstones, although in need of surface repair here and there, sell for millions of dollars, and Boston has become a major tourist destination with much to offer the gay and lesbian traveler. Among its chief attractions: a liberal environment (e.g., anti-bias laws), lots of history and culture (museums, music, theater, dance); and easy access to Provincetown, Ogunquit, and the mountains of Northern New England.

First-time visitors are often surprised to discover that Boston is actually quite small—barely 600,000 puritanical little souls live within the city limits, fewer than in San Antonio or Baltimore. It's also a young city thanks to the nearly 100 colleges and universities located in the metropolitan area. Indeed, perhaps the most frequent complaint I've heard about the city is that too many young people live here.

Boston is also rather conservative and provincial. One indication: I can't think of a single street or neighborhood I'd feel comfortable walking down holding my lover's hand, whereas on San Francisco's Castro Street, or even in nearby Provincetown, no one would look twice. Another provincial note: don't expect to disco and dine all night long. The Puritanical "blue laws" still exert an influence: restaurants start setting up for lunch around 11:30 pm, even on a Sat night, and last call in bars is 2 am. So there you have it: young, provincial, historic.

The South End, roughly bounded east-west by Arlington Street and Massachusetts Avenue, and north-south by the Orange Line park and Albany Street, has evolved into Boston's gay stronghold. Gay men and lesbians live everywhere, from the Fenway to Back Bay, from Beacon Hill to Brighton, but the largest concentration of gay Bostonians has settled in this slowly-gentrifying area. A financial crisis in the 1860's turned the South End into an instant slum soon after it was completed; it took 100 years for it to approach its intended status as a middle-class district. What you see today is the result of scores of gay and straight home-steaders, some of them African-American, Chinese, and Latino, who bought up Victorian shells by the block and restored them to their bay-windowed splendor. Gays also live in Bay Village, a postage-stamp enclave bordered by the South End and Back Bay (it was the main gay district in the forties and fifties), and Jamaica Plain, which has become quite popular with lesbians over the last few years, and has several trendy restaurants. Gay and lesbian Bostonians who can afford it prefer to live in Back Bay and Beacon Hill. These more pristine and less racial-ly-mixed high-rent districts are the city's most attractive (they're the ones the postcard photographers are always snapping) and historically have held their value better than the South End or other locales.

18

GETTING AROUND

Boston is a walking city, so you needn't rent a car unless you're planning to visit Provincetown, the Berkshires, or the White Mountains. When your feet give way, take the cheap and relatively safe "T," the USA's oldest public transit system. The ride in from Boston's Logan Airport takes 10-40 minutes depending on traffic. A free shuttle bus takes you to the Airport Station on the Blue Line; from there it's a 15-minute ride into town.

BEST TIME TO COME

Spring and Fall are ideal, but in this college-glutted town avoid the weeks centering around graduation, homecoming, parent's weekends, the Boston Marathon, and the Head of the Charles regatta.

STAY

GAY

Chandler Inn Hotel (26 Chandler St, South End; 800-842-3450/482-3450). Within easy walking distance of anywhere you'd want to go, 56 utilitarian but not tatty rooms with small bathrooms. Room 808 has best views (all "08" rooms are on the corner). Friendly staff. Popular night spot off lobby (see Fritz, below). Rates: $89-$99 double.

Oasis Guest House (22 Edgerly Rd, 267-2262). In the Fenway (border-ing Back Bay, not quite as conveniently located as the Chandler); most of the 15 rooms have private baths. Rates: $54-$82 double.

BEST BEDS

Boston's three best hotels, all with recommendable restaurants and impeccable service, are the **Ritz Carlton** (15 Arlington St, 800-241-3333); the **Four Seasons** (200 Boylston St, 338-4400), the only hotel in New York or New England to receive the Mobil Five Diamond Award); and the **Boston Harbor Hotel** (70 Rowes Wharf, 439-7000). At none of them will a staff member bat an eyelash if you request one big bed for the two of you. Weekend package rates are often available; call the hotels directly to find out.

SEE/DO

TEN THINGS NO SELF-RESPECTING GAY PERSON SHOULD MISS

The Boston Public Library. Full of hidden treasures, including the Sargeant Gallery, with murals painted by John Singer Sargeant, and the oasis-like Central Courtyard, the perfect place to rest after a long day of sightseeing.

The Gibson House (137 Beacon St, Back Bay, 267-6338). One of Boston's three historic homes (four, if you count the Gardner, below) that have been turned into museums. Rumor has it that the last Gibson, a bachelor, was, you know, special. Tours are provided, call for exact opening hours.

Nichols House Museum (55 Mt. Vernon St, Beacon Hill, 227-6993). Here Rose Nichols—writer, landscape architect, and niece of Saint-Gaudens, the sculptor—lived until she died at age 88.

The Isabella Stewart Gardner Museum (2 Palace Rd, Fenway, 566-1401). Important art collection in an ornate mansion modeled on a 15th century Venetian palace. Intimate concerts, too (734-1359 for schedules).

The Museum of Fine Arts (465 Huntington Ave, Fenway, 267-9300). World-class, could easily absorb a day.

The Boston Symphony Orchestra or the **Boston Pops** (266-1492). Tickets often available at short notice from the box office.

Day trip to Ogunquit, Maine (see **Resorts** section).

Crane's Beach, Ipswich. Pristine, limited-access beach preserve 45 minutes by car from Boston. Popular gay section (at the farthest end of the beach, naturally).

Provincetown (see under "The Resorts"). Possible as a day trip by car, plane, or ferry, but it's wiser to stay overnight.

Cruise the Esplanade. On summer afternoons, come to this Back Bay park along the Charles River and watch guys with their shirts off rollerblading and tanning.

Take a walk. Not only is it cheap, it's the best way to see this quintessential walking city. Wander along Mt. Vernon and Chestnut Streets on Beacon Hill, then cross into the Public Garden and down Commonwealth Avenue from Arlington to Gloucester Streets, especially in spring when the magnolias are in bloom. Then see the South End, America's largest continuous Victorian neighborhood. Union, Concord and Rutland Squares are especially fine streets.

20   NEAR BOSTON: OGUNQUIT, ME (AREA CODE 207)

Boston is unique among U.S. cities in that it has two gay seaside resorts within driving distance. Just 75 min from Boston, Ogunquit is by far the smaller of the two (see **Provincetown** under **Resorts** for the larger one). Don't expect Ogunquit to be nearly as gay as Provincetown, though. Nor is it a year-round destination: everything closes down for the winter. It is quieter, however, and closer to Boston. Lodging choices include the pet-friendly, gay-owned **Yellow Monkey Guest House** (44 Main St, Route 1, 646-9056, rates: $65-$90 in season, $40-$65 off) and **Tall Chimneys** (94 Main St, 646-8974, rates: call). For dancing, the only option is **The Club** (13 Main St, 646-6655), a dance and video bar.

KEEP FIT/RECREATION

Boston's gay men frequent two gay-owned gyms. Both offer excellent aerobics.

Metropolitan Health Club (209 Columbus Ave, 536-3006). Convenient, and 90% or more gay. Day fee: $10.

Mike's Gym (1A Waltham St, South End, 338-6677). Better equipped, more serious and less cruisy than the Metropolitan; less gay, more ethnically diverse crowd, but less convenient location—a 15 minute walk from the Chandler Inn. Day fee: $10.

EAT

TRES GAY

Club Café (209 Columbus Ave at Berkeley St, South End, 536-0966). Boston's main gay complex—restaurant, gym, cabaret, bar, and dance club—it was a revelation when it opened in 1980. Boston had never seen a place like this—nightly entertainment, white table cloths, candlelight, and above-average food—and indeed I didn't find anything like it in my travels to other cities. Snub Cafe, as it is affectionately known, is still a stylish spot, and although they're constantly tinkering with the decor and menu, and the food is up and down (up right now), this is the first place I bring an out-of-town visitor. The adjacent bar is Boston's most intimate, although it's small (see under nightlife). Entrees: $9-$18.

Geoffrey's (578 Tremont St, 266-1122). Friendly service, but the people- watching is better than the food. Salads, sandwiches, and entrees like pan- seared duck breast with fresh herbs. Entrees: $7-$15.

21

Mario's (69 Church St, 542-3776) has a 95% gay clientele. Basic Italian food, low prices. Slightly unattractive decor, but a gay institution since 1931. Entrees: $6.50-$15.

On the Park (375 Shawmut Ave, South End, 426-0862). Eclectic international. This lesbian-owned store-front operation is sometimes packed to its cozy little walls with Suburbanites on Safari, respectable folks from Newton looking for adventure; but guests are perfectly comfortable being who they are no matter what the clientele. No reservations. Brunch is a mob scene, especially on Sun. Not many lesbians, to chef/owner Lisa Martel's consternation. Entrees: $9-$14.

Tremont Ice Cream (584 Tremont St, South End, 247-8414). Convenient place to catch a quick breakfast or lunch. Get cozy in a booth and scan the small room and busy Tremont St. Everything under $6.

224 Boston Street (224 Boston St, Dorchester, 265-1217). Not within walking distance of anything, but worth the drive. Fun, friendly atmosphere. Gay owned and operated, eclectic food, a place where you'll feel comfortable stealing a kiss. Entrees: $7-$17.

GAY-FRIENDLY

Any of the restaurants in the South End are gay-friendly.

Botolph's on Tremont (569 Tremont St, South End, 424-8577). Inexpensive and mostly gay. Entrees: $6-$14.

Icarus (3 Appleton St, South End, 426-1790). Gay-owned South End institution with national following and the best food of the gay-oriented dining spots. Brunch gayer than most other meals; more gay later in the evening, too. Sat is suburban night out. Lobster over squid ink papparadelle with roasted red peppers is typical of the enticing fare. Entrees: $17-23.

TOP TABLES

Recently, Boston experienced a restaurant explosion, with lots of new names and menus. But the city boasts four restaurants of less recent vintage that attract national attention—the kinds of places with menu descriptions like, "Little caviar and ham sandwiches in a puddle of watercress aioli." Most have noise levels reminiscent of a junior high school cafeteria, and the waiters give attitude. They are: **Biba** (272 Boylston St, Back Bay, 426-7878); **Hammersley's** (553 Tremont St, South End, 423-2700); **Olive's** (10 City Sq, 242-1999); **Seasons Restaurant** at the Bostonian Hotel (across from Quincy Market, 523-3600).

PLAY/MEET

Boston/Cambridge has about two dozen gay bars and discos, most of them well-patronized and busy. Unlike other cities, Boston's club scene doesn't change with the wind. Most of these places have been around for years and are scattered throughout Boston and Cambridge, so if you're bar-hopping you'll need a car or a cab.

MOSTLY FOR DANCING

Avalon on Sunday nights (15 Lansdowne St, Fenway, 262-2424). Lansdowne is an out-of-the-way street near Fenway Park, where the Sox play. Cavernous Avalon has the largest dance floor in the city.

Campus/Man Ray (21 Brookline St, Central Sq, Cambridge, 864-0406). One of these split personality clubs—two, two, two clubs in one. You cross from one area to the other and it's like Alice Through the Looking Glass. Very young crowd (is anyone checking ID's here?), latest trendy music. Call to find out which nights are all gay/lesbian.

Chaps (27-31 Huntington Ave, Back Bay, 266-7778). Within walking distance of everywhere. It's been here forever. There are three bars, some video, and exotic dancers some nights. Mostly men, mostly younger, it's fairly upscale and attracts a comely crowd—some say the best looking men in Boston.

Quest (1270 Boylston St, Fenway, 424-7747). Dancing/video bar formerly called 1270, attracting a youngish crowd. Several levels, including an open rooftop terrace in summer. Sat is the big gay night.

MOSTLY FOR DRINKING/CRUISING

Club Cafe/Moonshine (209 Columbus Ave, South End, 536-0966). Great place to stop for a drink after work or a day of sightseeing, but don't expect to meet anyone in this rather reserved climate. Mostly for ladies on Sat nights.

Fritz (26 Chandler St, South End, adjacent to Chandler Inn, 482-4428). Neighborhood place, with a non-attitudinal South End crowd; Sun pms are the prime time. Age group 25 and up, most in mid-30's early 40's. Sports on TV. Opens 12 noon. Table service.

23

Jacques (79 Broadway, Bay Village, 338-9066). Long-running piano bar with drag shows.

Paradise (180 Mass. Ave, Cambridge, 864-4130). While you're checking out Campus, try this lively, been-there-for-years bar with go-go boys located just over the Charles. The ads promise "fierce men, hot tribal and gogo whores" every Thu, Fri, and Sat. Upstairs there's a bar; downstairs there's a bar with a small dance floor.

Playland (21 Essex St, 338-7254). In the so-called "Combat Zone," this interesting place attracts working boys and their customers.

AFTER-HOURS

The Loft (Stanhope St, South End). Tiny place that doesn't advertise. Used to be a sex joint, now just dancing (no liquor license). Gets going at 2 am when the other bars close.

PIANO BAR

Napoleon Club (52 Piedmont St, Bay Village, 338-7547). Show tunes, French whore house decor, older men singing around a baby grand while a woman who looks like Marie Antoinette on a bad hair day twinkles the ivories. Upstairs, a small disco called **Josephine's** can be fun on Sat nights.

LEATHER

Boston Eagle (520 Tremont St, South End, 482-4428). Boston's idea of hyper-masculine leather bars is relatively tame. Convenient South End location, an attractive place supposedly for leather and Levis people, but they let anyone in.

119 Merrimac St (119 Merrimac St, North End, 367-0713). Levis, leather, motorcycle crowd.

Ramrod (1254 Boylston St, Fenway, 266-2986). Although this is for the Levis and leather crowd, it's an easy place to meet and mingle. Doesn't get moving until after 10 pm.

SEX CLUB

For something less savory, even puritanical Boston permits a sex club here and there.

Safari Club (90 Wareham St, South End, 292-0011). Open 24 hours a day—a sex club cum gym that the neighbors are trying to shut down.

SHOP

Marquis (73 Berkeley St, South End, 426-2120). Formerly Little Shop of Horrors. Only in Boston would you have such a store: Leather and latex sold in an atmosphere of burning incense and classical music. Cards, gifts, videos, condoms.

Newbury Street. Boston's trendiest shopping promenade runs the length of the Back Bay and is full of unique, non-chain boutiques, a relief in this homogenized shopping world of ours where the same signs stare out at you from Sioux City to Singapore.

Louis (Corner of Newbury and Berkeley Sts, 262-6100). Boston-only clothing emporium for men and women. Lots of good-looking sales associates.

Copley Place (Dartmouth St). Toniest shopping mall in town.

Filene's Basement, the original, is still worth a visit.

RESOURCES

GENERAL INFORMATION

Boston Convention and Visitors Bureau (536-4100).

Newcomer's Handbook™ **for Boston** (First Books, 312-276-5911).
Tremendously useful book for anyone (gay or straight) *moving* here.

GAY/HIV INFORMATION

The AIDS Action Committee (437-6200). Among the oldest and most
active AIDS organizations in the US.

BOOKSTORES

Glad Day Bookshop (673 Boylston St, Back Bay, 267-3010). One of
the better G&L bookstores in the country (after all, this is bookish
Boston). Video rentals.

We Think the World of You (540 Tremont St, 423-1965). Relatively
new, classy store-front operation with helpful staff in convenient South
End location. Mostly gay, but some mainstream, titles.

PUBLICATIONS

Bay Windows (266-6670). The more serious weekly newspaper.

IN (426-8246). Has evolved from a party rag to a more earnest contender.

CHICAGO

WHAT TO EXPECT

Here's Chicago, the short form. People like to live here. Despite the grim winters, they're not plotting their escape to Portland or San Francisco. Two reasons: the inexpensive but high-quality housing and the friendly people. Bouncers and even subway clerks smile and say hello and thank-you. Chicago is a fun place, too. Whereas Boston and Washington tend to shut down as the night rolls on, the Windy City offers lots of late-night life and a wide choice of gay bars and clubs.

27

This is a city of livable neighborhoods and exemplary architecture. People revere architects here the way they do sports heroes in other cities. The man on the street can tell a Mies van der Rohe from a Phillip Johnson, and will have an opinion about it. But make no mistake: in this sports-crazed town everyone worships jocks too, and there are gay bowling and softball leagues out the ying yang.

A few other distinguishing marks: there's less emphasis on looks and status here than on the East Coast, where the "A-list/B-list" mentality reigns. Things flow at a distinctly home-spun, corn-fed, Midwest pace. Gay folks here aren't as slick as they are in NY or LA.

Queer ground zero is the triangle defined by N. Halsted, N. Clark, and Belmont. The gay area is known as Boystown, although you also hear "Wrigleyville" and "Lakeview" used. But as gentrification progresses and rents go up, gays and lesbians move on. Andersonville, further north on N. Clark, is becoming popular with nesting couples, although single boys still like Boystown. Many gays live in the suburbs of Chicago. Suburban Oak Park became the first town in Illinois to institute domestic partner benefits for city employees, and all of Cook County enjoys anti-bias legislation. Lots of gay bars vie for trade in area code 708—places like Oak Park, Forest Park, Schaumburg and Calumet. And there's a gay/lesbian presence in Bloomingdale, IL, 30 miles from Chicago, with its cutely-preserved downtown. There are even suburban gay associations.

BEST TIME TO COME

Anytime but winter.

GETTING AROUND

You'll need a car only if you're doing a Frank Lloyd Wright pilgrimage or you want to see the fabulous North Shore suburbs where they filmed *Ordinary People* and *Risky Business*. Rapid transit will take you wherever else you need to go—$1.50 a pop.

STAY

28

GAY

You can choose from two gay guest houses, but for the same money you get a private bath at one of the budget gay-friendly hotels listed below.

Villa Toscana (3447 N. Halsted, 404-2643). Right in the middle of the action, but surprisingly quiet. Attractive little house set back in a big yard. Three bright rooms share one bath, and all have hardwood floors, TV and air, but no phones. Rates: $69 weekdays, $79 weekends, including in-room breakfast.

Magnolia Place (5353 Magnolia Ave, 334-6860). Small guest house in Andersonville, which is becoming a gay enclave in its own right. Casual management attitude. Three rooms share a bath. Rates: $60 single, $70 double.

GAY-FRIENDLY

City Suites Hotel (933 W. Belmont, 404-3400). Located in Boystown near rapid transit and the popular Berlin club, this low-cost alternative hotel is decent enough, but on my visit the hallways smelled (oil fumes?) and the carpeting was worn. Rates: $75-$89.

Days Inn (644 W. Diversey, 525-7010). Central location, low rates, new carpeting and furnishings. Rates: $69-$89 (sometimes lower during late fall and winter).

BEST BEDS

There are no luxury establishments within walking distance of Boystown. For that you'll have to stay downtown, which might not be such a bad idea. Both the **Nikko** (320 N. Dearborn St, 1-800-NIKKO-US) at $160 for a room-with-a-view and the **Inter-Continental** (505 N. Michigan Ave, 1-800-628-2112) at about $150, offer superior fitness centers as well as convenient Loop locations.

SEE/DO

TEN THINGS NO SELF-RESPECTING GAY PERSON SHOULD MISS

Belmont Rocks area. In warm weather, great place to watch gay men who sun on the huge boulders. Take Belmont east until you hit Lake Michigan and ask someone for directions.

Wrigley Field. If you're at all sports-minded, watch the Cubs from the bleachers. Even if the game isn't that hot, the shirtless straight boys are.

Gerber-Hart Gay and Lesbian Library/Archives (3352 N. Paulina, 883-3003). A wonderful collection of gay ephemera, newspapers, historical documents, books, and other resources.

Gay theater. Lots of improv comedy and other gay-themed rep theatricals. Try the Bailiwick Rep (1225 W. Belmont, 883-1090), Upstart Theatre (1139 W. Flourndy, 226-8185), or Party Productions (327-5252) whose long-running comedy *Party* may still be on.

Architecture. Take the Architecture River Cruise given by the Chicago Architecture Foundation (922-3432). Walking tours also offered (224 S. Michigan Ave, 922-TOUR).

Frank Lloyd Wright. Tour his creations (private homes and the Unity Temple) and former home and studio (951 Chicago Ave, 708-848-1500) in Oak Park. Visit Pride Agenda Bookstore (see below) while you're there. Also tour the Robie House (5757 S. Woodlawn St, 702-8374).

Bahai House of Worship (100 Linden Ave, Wilmette, 708-256-4400). Free tours of this inspiring religious building.

Sears Tower Skydeck (Jackson St bet. Wacker and Franklin, 875-9696). Might as well say you've scaled the world's tallest building.

The Field Museum (Roosevelt Rd at Lake Shore Dr, 922-9410). Unique natural history museum.

Art Institute of Chicago (111 S. Michigan Ave, 443-3600). World-class home of Seurat's *Sunday Afternoon on the Island of La Grande Jatte* and Wood's *American Gothic* among other major must-sees.

NEAR CHICAGO: SAUGATUCK, MICHIGAN (AREA CODE 616)

Just two hours from Chicago on the sandy shores of eastern Lake Michigan, this popular summer getaway (really two communities—Saugatuck and Douglas—with a year-round population of about 2,500) is the Midwest's Provincetown or Key West. In winter, cross-country skiing is popular (there's a fairly lively off-season business). During the day in summer, sunning on **Oval Beach** is the main activity. (The gay section is on the adjacent private beach; small admission charged). Gay central is the **Douglas Dunes** (333 Blue Star Highway, Douglas, 857-1401), a complex like Key West's Atlantic Shores, with bar, disco, cabaret, and outdoor space. Here you'll find 22 motel rooms and 8 cottages sleeping up to six; in season rates start at $60 and go up to $340 for the 3-night July 4 weekend; cottages also available. Across the street is the straight-owned but predominantly gay 27-room **Lighthouse** (857-2271, rates: $85 week off season, $75-$110 in, holidays more). Other choices include: the 8-room **Kirby House B&B** (294 W. Center St, Douglas, $90-$115; 857-2904) and the 3-room. gay-owned **Alpen Haus** (41 Spring St, 857-1119, rates: $50-$70 off, $65-$85 in season). When stomachs start to growl, head for **Cafe Sir Douglas** (part of Douglas Dunes, entrees $10-$20) or across the street to greasy spoon **Kalico Kitchen** (312 Blue Star Hwy, 857-2678, entrees $4-$11). For a special meal, try the authentic country French cuisine at **Restaurant Toulouse** (248 Culver St, 857-1561, entrees: $13-$19), where about 25% of the patrons are gay on any given summer evening. Getting there: take I-90/94 from Chicago, to the Saugatuck/Douglas exit. For free info: the **Saugatuck/Douglas Visitors Bureau** (857-1701).

SPECIAL EVENTS

NortHalsted Market Days is an annual street fair held during the last week of July or first week in August. 883-0500 for info.

The **International Mr. Leather** contest and a number of gay sports competitions happen every Memorial Day weekend.

KEEP FIT/RECREATION

Oddly, there is no really gay-friendly or gay-owned full-service health club in Chi-town. Some gays go to Bally's Chicago Health Club, which did not take day guests; in any case, I found the management unhelpful. Here's what else I found.

Lehman Sports Club (2700 N. Lehman Ct, 871-8300). For a large gay clientele and excellent facilities in gay central, this is your best bet. Probably 40%-50% of the men are gay, 50% straight female. Lots of the latest cardio equipment, excellent aerobics, a full line each of Nautilus and Cybex, plus a decent amount of free weights all in 25,000 sq. ft. Friendly staff. Day fee: $15.

Chicago Body Shop (3246 N. Halsted, 248-7717). Above a bath house, this is a small gym with mostly free weights. Not very attractive, but it's the only all-gay gym in town. Day fee: $8.

EAT

TRES GAY

Lots of gay-frequented and gay-owned dining here. Pity about the food, which in most cases isn't great.

Buddies (3301 N. Clark, 477-4066). Adjacent to bar of same name (see below). Best burgers in town, including a yummy veggie burger. Solid comfort food like smothered pork chops, with $5.95 specials mid-week, and $1 draft beer specials. George (a grandfather at 44, as he'll readily admit) and his longtime companion Marty (also a grampa) are the friendly owners, and make this a logical first stop on your tour. Entrees: everything under $10.

Cornelia's (750 W. Cornelia, 248-8333). A healthy portion of attitude comes with every meal at this very (90%?) gay eatery with a pleasant patio. Locals say the food is inconsistent. Entrees: $10-$15.

Cucina Bella (543 W Diversey, 868-1119). Relatively new, gay-owned Italian; draws lots of boys. Entrees: $6-$14.

Dellwood Pickle (1475 W. Balmoral, 271-7728). Inexpensive store front dining, decent food such as blackened chicken breast or catfish and fresh pastas. Gay, artsy crowd, kind of retro hippy. Entrees: $7-$9.

Genesee Depot (3736 N. Broadway, 528-6990). I didn't try this BYOB/ no reservations eatery, but everyone says the food is sensational with choices like shrimp Creole and breast of Peking duck. Not an attractive space. Entrees: $11-$18.

Las Mananitas (3523 N. Halsted, 528-2109). Hard surfaces and bad art, but a place for cheap, decent Mexican food such as deep-fried red snapper, in the company of a gay crowd. Entrees: $6-$15.

Oo-La-La (3335 N. Halsted, 935-7708). Too-trendy for its own good, our sources say. Long waits for tables, overpriced, they know they're hot and they treat you that way. And it's not as gay-clienteled as others listed here. Still, some swear by the food, which includes stand-by linguine with clams, and penne with smoked eggplant. Entrees: $9-$16.

Roscoe's (3354 N. Halsted, 281-3355). Perfectly fine sandwiches, salads, soups, and other simple but tasty fare. On summer weekends, they put tables on the sidewalk, and this is *the* place to see and be seen. No credit cards. Entrees: most under $6.

Scooters (1725 W. Balmoral, 561-2765). Gay-owned coffee house in the Andersonville area, convenient to the Magnolia Place guest house. They serve light food, and are very accommodating. Nice place to hang.

GAY FRIENDLY

32

Mia Francesca (3311N. Clark, 281-3310). This sublime gay-friendly but mostly straight-clienteled eatery dishes out the best chow in Wrigleyville. Volume levels like your junior high cafeteria, but the stylish decor and crowd and inexpensive prices more than compensate. No reservations, so people start lining up at 5 pm, even on Mon nights. Entrees: $9-$16.

TOP TABLES

Ambria (2300 N. Lincoln Pk W, 472-5959) and **Carlos'** (429 Temple Ave, Highland Park, 708-432-0770) are often ranked as two of Chicago's best restaurants.

PLAY/MEET

There are something like 100 gay bars in Chicago and the immediate suburbs, including four major leather bars. But not a lot of sex clubs like you'd find in New York.

MOSTLY FOR DANCING

Berlin (954 W. Belmont, 348-4975). Hip dance club with a little bit of everything—gays and open-minded straights, men and women, black and white. Not a place to come alone or to cruise. Some nights there are videos and gorgeous male dancers, who are there just as backdrop—people are too busy dancing to notice.

G.L.E.E. Club (1543 N. Kingsbury, 243-2075). The place for dancing on Sun nights (starting at 10). Known as **Crobar** other nights.

Vortex (3631 N. Halsted, 975-6622, hotline 975-0660). *The* major dance palace. Warehouse-like, it attracts a lot of 708-ers (the Chicago equivalent of NYC's Bridge and Tunnel crowd). Great sound and light system.

MOSTLY FOR CRUISING/DRINKING

Big Chicks (5024 N. Sheridan Rd, 728-5511). Tons of fun but out of the way, with eclectic music and crowd—men, women, gay, straight, young, old. Welcoming and worth the trip.

Buddies (3301 N. Clark, 477-4066). Probably the friendliest place in town—the gay Cheers—with a good-value restaurant adjacent. On the small side. If you can't feel at home here, you won't anywhere. Mixed age group, some women.

Roscoe's (3354 N. Halsted, 281-3355). The city's most popular guppie dance bar, tavern, cafe, and game room. this is the kind of place you can take your parents to. The owner's collection of antique doll houses, toys, and memorabilia adds considerable class to this unique spot. Fun young crowd, but probably not a place to come alone since this is a stand-and-model crowd. Nice outdoor spaces, jammed on Sun pms.

33

Sidetrack (3349 N. Halsted, 477-9189). Right across the street from Roscoe's—people joke that someone should build a tunnel between the two. This attractive space (warm wood contrasted with high-techy galvanized steel) ranks as the premier guppie video bar in town. Patrons stand around and watch amusing videos. Comedy nights, sing-a-longs, and games occur each week on a rotating basis that hasn't changed for years: Mon: show tune sing-along. Tue: C&W. Wed: Music of the 50s, 60s, and 70s. Thu: Comedy. Fri: a little bit of everything. Sat: retro. Packed on Sun pms, when, in summer, the roof deck is a mob scene.

PIANO BARS

Dandy's (3729 N. Halsted, 525-1200). Dull piano bar (karaoke some nights) with cute-but-not-friendly bartenders.

Gentry (712 N. Rush, 664-1033). Where the suits and conventioneers go after day is done. Video bar downstairs; upstairs there's a cabaret. Also a relatively new branch located at 3320 N. Halsted.

LESBIAN

Paris Dance (1122 W. Montrose, 769-0602). Currently the only place exclusively for women.

LEATHER

Cell Block (3702 N. Halsted, 665-8064). Hottest leather bar in the city.

Chicago Eagle (5015 N. Clark, 728-0050). The heavy leather bar. Dress code in the "Pit" downstairs. Leather shop on premises.

Manhole (3458 N. Halsted, 975-9244). How can they answer the phone with a straight face? "Thank you for calling Manhole, can I help you?" Three bars, porn videos, chain link fence. The "inner" bar, where much groping goes on during "Lights Out" and underwear parties is open only to leather-wearers and the shirtless on Fri and Sat nights.

SHOP

There's a *lot* of gay retail, so bring that plastic.

GIFTS AND GAY WEAR

Gallimaufry Gallery (3345 N. Halsted, 348-8090). One-of-a-kind gift-ware from around the world. Truly different.

Gay Mart (3457 N. Halsted, 929-4272). All the usual gay paraphernalia—cards, T's, fridge magnets, some books. Friendly owner.

He Who Eats Mud (3247 N. Broadway, 525-0616). Gay-owned and themed, the name was chosen out of a hat at a cocktail party (must have been a wild one). Best T-shirts in town, great cards and unique wrapping paper.

Pyramid Gifts (3021 N. Clark, 348-2658). Cards, candles, T-shirts, mugs with a gay twist.

We Are Everywhere (3434 N. Halsted, 404-0590). Exclusive gay-themed T-shirts, cards, the whole gay nine yards.

CLOTHES

Bad Boys (3311 N. Broadway, 549-7701). Great shirts, underwear, other cool clothing for men. Cute and helpful employees.

Hardwear (3243 N. Broadway, 296-0801). Tight, body-conscious duds for the gym-toned.

Marshall Field's (835 N. Michigan Ave, 335-7700). The men's department of this quintessential Chicago department store often offers some attractive male scenery. Snazzy clothes.

RESOURCES

GENERAL INFORMATION

The Chicago Convention and Tourism Bureau (2301 S. Lake Shore Drive, 60616, 567-8500). Ask for their "Official Visitors Guide."

Newcomer's Handbook™ for Chicago (First Books, 312-276-5911). Tremendously useful book for anyone (gay or straight) *moving* here.

GAY/HIV INFORMATION

Stop AIDS Chicago (909 W. Belmont, 871-3300).

BOOKSTORES

35

People Like Us (3321 N. Clark, 248-6363). Two really helpful owners, a gay man and a lesbian, run Chicago's only totally-gay/lesbian bookstore, and a great place for "concierge" information.

Pride Agenda Bookstore (1109 Westgate, Oak Park, 708-524-8429). Exclusively gay/lesbian, located in beautiful Oak Park.

Unabridged Books (3251 N. Broadway, 883-9119). Gay-owned and carries many gay titles, but not exclusively gay.

PUBLICATIONS

Lots of gay press. As in other cities, the listings are "selective"—only advertisers make it.

Gay Chicago (3121 N. Broadway, 60657, 327-7271). Biggest weekly, in magazine form. Features, news, nightlife, and a calendar.

Windy City Times (970 W. Montana, 935-1974). The "serious" paper.

Babble (3223 N. Sheffield, 248-4542). An irreverent party rag catering to Generation Q.

Nightlines (3059 N. Southport, Chicago 60657, 871-7610). Pocket-sized weekly with news, reviews, and club/bar info.

Then there are the "pink" pages. Look for:

Out! published by the Nightlines folks, and *The Alternative Phone Book* (425 W. Surf Street, 60657, 472-6319). Both list only advertisers.

DALLAS

AREA CODE 214

WHAT TO EXPECT

E ven before you leave Dallas' gargantuan international airport you sense that this city does things big. It takes so *long* to leave this Manhattan-sized aerodrome. No mere access road serves these terminals. Instead, there's a full fledged superhighway. You drive on this thing for miles, or so it seems, at 55 mph and you're *still* in Dallas Fort-Worth Airport. At the Budget Rent-a-Car counter, they're fielding the usual panicked calls from customers who can't find the car return area (there are no signs warning you to go into the parking lot first). The rumor in the rental car depot is that the master planner of this mess now twiddles his days away in an asylum somewhere in Europe, if that's any consolation.

Once you find your way into town, you quickly discover that sprawling Big-D, home to such corporate giants as Exxon, American Airlines, JC Penney, and, how could we forget, Mary Kay, is also a bustling magnet for gays and lesbians from throughout the Southwest. Dallas supports a large gay community. In fact, there are as many gay organizations here as you'd find in New York or Washington. Like to fly? Try the gay pilots association. Like to read? There's a lesbian book club. Nearly two dozen AIDS organizations compete for clients.

Despite all these groups—perhaps because Dallas is the "buckle of the Bible belt"—gays tend to keep a lower profile than they would in less conservative cities. One small indication of this reticence, perhaps, is that the city's exemplary gay men's chorus isn't called the "Dallas *Gay* Chorale" but rather the *Turtle Creek* Chorale. Even so, the city boasts what is perhaps the largest gay church in the country—the modern-looking Cathedral of Hope—and a lively gay and lesbian community center complete with credit union.

Suburban-like Oaklawn is gay central, and the crossroads of Cedar Springs and Throckmorton its epicenter. Here you'll find the most popular clubs, bars, shops, restaurants, and other attractions, along with great people-watching in the sidewalk cafes. Throughout Dallas, there are dozens of venues for every taste, and they're well-patronized. Even so, a prime way of meeting people is at large private parties held at home. These get-togethers—not for fundraising, just for fun—are a great way for newcomers to make friends. Another way to meet is less genteel: at all hours of the day and night, men drive to various parks and cruise each other *en voiture*. It's like going to the baths, except instead of wearing a towel you wear a car.

You'll probably come here for business rather than tourism. Dallas is rapidly developing into a major convention destination and corporate headquarters city, but its tourist attractions leave something to be desired. This isn't Boston or San Francisco. There are few old homes to view, and no historic districts, unless you count Deep Ellum. As one local explained to me, "When something gets historic, we tear it down." Still, Dallas is worth a visit, if only because the men are so friendly and so darn cute.

GETTING THERE

Dallas is served by the enormous DFW megaport. Super Shuttle offers door-to-door van service for about $14.

GETTING AROUND

Rent a car. Everyone drives everywhere here.

STAY

GAY

The Inn on Fairmount (3701 Fairmount, 522-2800). One of the best-run and best-looking urban gay guest houses in the country. Everything is new and clean and tastefully decorated, plus the host, former IBM executive Michael McVay, loves what he's doing and it shows. Seven rooms, all with private bath, individual phone line, and color TV but no VCR. Includes breakfast with homemade muffins. Rates: $80-$120.

BEST BEDS

The Mansion on Turtle Creek (2821 Turtle Creek Blvd, 559-2100). Still the city's—some say the country's—best hotel, within walking distance of the gay district. You'll never arrive here without being promptly met by a valet, even if there's a horde checking in, nor is it likely you'll walk through the front door without it being opened for you. Plus there's that awesome restaurant (see **Eat**, below). Rates: $195 (weekend)-$275 (corporate).

BUDGET CHOICE

The Melrose Hotel (3015 Oaklawn, 800-MELROSE). Top choice for something affordable and right in the heart of gay Dallas. Here you'll find

182 beautifully-restored rooms, complimentary transportation within a five mile radius and an excellent restaurant are additional incentives. Rates: $89 (weekends)-$125 (corporate).

SEE/DO

TEN THINGS NO SELF-RESPECTING GAY PERSON SHOULD MISS

Morton H. Meyerson Symphony Center (2301 Flora St, 670-3600). The I.M. Pei-designed home of the Dallas Symphony

Turtle Creek Chorale (520-ARTS for advance tickets or info). The city's gay chorus, definitely worth planning your visit around.

The Dallas Museum of Art (1717 N Harwood, 922-1200). While not of the same caliber as Chicago's Art Institute or New York's Metropolitan, definitely worth a visit, especially after recent expansion.

39

The Kimbell Art Museum (3333 Camp Bowie, Forth Worth, 817-654-1034). World-class museum. The building, designed by Louis Kahn, qualifies as a work of art in itself and, just as early observers feared, competes with the paintings hanging on its walls.

Deep Ellum area (747-DEEP). Wander in search of live music clubs and restaurants.

Highland Park and **White Rock Lake.** You can fill up an hour or so driving around these areas to see all the fabulous houses—there's a lot of money here, and people aren't afraid to flaunt it.

Lee Park. On Sun afternoons, check out the volleyball action.

That Special Blend (3307 Oaklawn, 522-3736). Watch the boys go by at this popular gay-central coffee bar.

The Sixth Floor (411 Elm, 653-6666). Formerly the Texas School Book Depository, is a sad and haunting must-see which examines JFK's life, death, and legacy. Even if you're not old enough to remember where you were when Kennedy was shot, consider bringing Kleenex.

SPECIAL EVENTS

Razzle Dazzle Dallas. Gay festival held every year in early May.

Texas Freedom Day Parade. Held in late Sep each year. With nearly 100 floats, celebrates the day when the Texas sodomy law was repealed.

KEEP FIT/RECREATION

Dallas' two main gay gyms are notable for their friendly clientele and staff.

Centrum Sports Club (3102 Oak Lawn in the Centrum Center, 522-4100). More mixed (gay/straight and male/female) and larger than Crossroads (below) with a big pool, aerobics, and squash courts. Lots of Texan beefcakes who flirt with out-of-towners. Day fee: $13.

Crossroads Gym (4001 Cedar Springs Road, 522-9376). On the small side, but it has everything most people need, including free weights and Stairmasters, and it's 99% gay and lesbian. A location right in the gay strip is a plus, too. Day fee: $9 ($17.50 for three consecutive days).

40

EAT

TRES GAY

The Black Eyed Pea (3857 Cedar Springs, 521-4580). This popular chain began here, now always packed with gays and lesbians. The menu consists of pot roast, pork chops, and other mom-type fare, all of it well under $10.

Lucky's Café (Oaklawn and Bowser, 522-3500). *The* place for ogling a parade of cute Dallas men and women during Sun brunch, with everything well under $10.

The Bronx (3835 Cedar Springs, 521-5821). A non-chain low-cost eatery with so-so food. Entrees: $8-$15.

Hunky's (4000 Cedar Springs, 522-1212). A better choice where all the burgers and sandwiches cost less than $5.

Spasso Pizza and Pasta (4000 Cedar Springs, 521-1141). Inexpensive and gay, although straight-owned and operated. Entrees: everything under $8.

TOP TABLES

Dallas is blessed with some of the best restaurants in the country, at least if you like Southwestern flavors. **The Restaurant, Mansion on Turtle Creek** (2821 Turtle Creek Blvd, 559-2100, entrees around $30) is where I'd want my last meal on earth. **Star Canyon** (3102 Oaklawn Ave in the Centrum complex, 520-STAR, entrees: $14-$18) is a dazzling newcomer with Steve Pyles at the helm.

PLAY/MEET

As befits the country's seventh largest city, there are clubs and bars here for every taste—well over 30 of them, in fact. Most places close at 2 am, when the alcohol stops flowing, and are located on Cedar Springs at the epicenter of gay Dallas, or, less conveniently, in dreary strip malls a mile or two away.

MOSTLY FOR DANCING

The Village Station (3911 Cedar Springs, 380-3808). Premier dance club, especially on Sat and Sun nights when they line up for blocks to pay the hefty cover. Predictably, the crowd is young and frisky. Recently expanded into a club next door.

MOSTLY FOR DRINKING/CRUISING

Anchor Inn (4024 Cedar Springs, 526-4098). Fishing nets and other unattractive nautical paraphernalia; right next door and interconnected to Big Daddy's (see below) and Numbers. Famous for its male dancers, three shows daily. A bit trashy.

Big Daddy's (4024 Cedar Springs, 528-4098). Drag shows. Decor won't win any prizes from *Architectural Digest.*

Brick Bar (4117 Maple, 521-2024). Especially on Sat nights, the leather & Levis set flocks here.

Crews Inn (3215 N. Fitzhugh, 526-9510) . Everyone comes here on Tue nights. Near Zippers.

JR's Bar & Grill (3923 Cedar Springs, 380-3808). Picture-windowed, tin-ceilinged bar full of Dallas' stand-and-model preppies. Way above-average decor.

Moby Dick's (4011 Cedar Springs, 520-MOBY). Pretty LA-look crowd. Happening place with industrial decor, good music, lots of videos, and really good-looking bartenders.

Throckmorton Mining Company (3014 Throckmorton, 380-3808). Friendly but very dark, low-ceilinged bar popular with bears and their cubs and cunningly decorated in the latest neon beer signs. Said to be the least racially-segregated of the town's watering holes.

Round-up (3912 Cedar Springs, 522-9611). For C&W aficionados.

Zippers (3333 N. Fitzhugh, 526-9519). Rhymes with strippers—what a coincidence. A claustrophobic, dark and smoky dive, but it has its charms, or at least the strippers do.

PIANO BARS

The Hideaway (4144 Buena Vista, 559-2966). Offers entertainment such as drag shows and cabaret acts; large outdoor patio.

John L's (2525 Wycliff, 520-2525). Quality entertainment, including Tue night comedy.

LEATHER

42

Dallas Eagle (behind the 7-11 at Inwood and Maple, 357-4345). Popular new leather bar.

LESBIANS

Sue Ellen's (3903 Cedar Springs, 380-3808). Sharp-looking lesbian bar (men welcome) with glass block decor near the center of things. Restaurant booths line one wall.

SHOP

MALLS

Dallas boasts more shopping centers per capita than any US city, including America's oldest, **Highland Park Village** (Mockingbird Lane and Preston Rd).

Northpark Center (Northwest Hwy and N. Central Expwy). Where the gay boys shop.

The Galleria (LBJ Freeway and the Dallas Parkway). Contains all the prestige names like Vuitton and Gucci.

GAY SHOPS

Nuvo (3900 Cedar Springs, 522-6886). Unusual homeware, furniture, books, and cards in the "Crossroads" area.

Union Jack (3920 Cedar Springs, 528-9600). Place to go for casual clothing and a haircut.

Lobo (4008-C Cedar Springs, 522-1132). Gay paraphernalia, rents and sells x-rated videos, and carries some gay magazines.

Babylon (4008-D Cedar Springs, 522-5887). Features the work of local gay artists, including jewelry, chimes, clothing, and frames.

Shades of Gray (3928 Cedar Springs, 521-GREY). Everything leather.

RESOURCES

GENERAL INFORMATION

Lesbian Info Line (528-2426).

Gay and Lesbian Community Center (2701 Reagan, 528-4233).

Dallas Convention & Visitors Bureau (746-6677).

GAY/HIV INFORMATION

There are dozens of AIDS organizations.

AIDS Resource Center (2701 Reagan, 521-5124). Provides emergency assistance, educational materials, and more.

AIDS Services of Dallas (800 N. Lancaster, 941-0523). Operates two licensed facilities for long and short term care.

PUBLICATIONS

The Dallas Voice (3000 Carlisle St, Suite 200, Dallas 75204, 754-8711). Weekly gay rag.

This Week in Texas (3300 Reagan St, Dallas 75219, 520-TWIT). Weekly covering Dallas and other Texan cities; back issues $2. Both are distributed free in bars.

BOOKSTORE

Crossroads Market & Bookstore (3930 Cedar Springs, 521-8919). The major gay bookstore in town; offers a thoughtful selection of publications.

New Orleans

WHAT TO EXPECT

Bawdy, steamy, elegantly decaying New Orleans gets my vote for the fun capital of the world—at least the gay world. No other city is so dedicated to the art of partying—24 hours a day, 365 days a year. French and Spanish explorers and missionaries first settled New Orleans, beginning in 1699 when the French inhabited an outpost. Jean-Baptiste le Moyne, Sieur de Bienville, officially established the city in 1718. The Spanish took over in 1769, the French gained control from them in 1801, and the U.S. bought the whole thing in 1803—the famous Louisiana Purchase. Between the War of 1812 and the War Between the States, New Orleans enjoyed its "Golden Age." The industrialization of the North, the end of slavery, and the advent of rail (which made river transport less important), all contributed to the city's economic decline. Oil briefly rallied to the Big Easy's rescue, but the city has yet to recover from the bust of the 1980's. Today, racial and economic tension has led to a staggering murder rate. Be advised that you're more likely to get mugged here than in most cities described in this book. When leaving clubs late at night do so in a group or take a cab.

And be careful when entering Tom Long's card shop/hair salon on Bourbon Street. He may add you to his x-rated snapshot collection (ask him to show it to you). "I'm a party animal and a major league tramp, and that's why I love New Orleans," he proclaims. "I love it because it's laid back, it's a 24-hours-a-day town." But he warns, "This place will chew you up and spit you out in no time at all. You have to know when to quit or you'll get burned out real fast." His warning has the ring of truth. This is a decadent town, where a combination of drugs and alcohol leads to hazy judgment. Bars don't place bowls of rubbers within easy reach as they do in other cities, and one merchant who sells condoms says that demand is low. "We'll all probably be dead in ten years," Long offers with a touch of *je ne give a damn pas.*

Meanwhile, everyone is having fun. Gays live throughout New Orleans, but ground zero is most definitely in the bustling French Quarter, although gay life goes on elsewhere in the city as well. What's interesting is that the gay clubs are so visible—not hidden down alleyways, or sequestered in windowless, dark caverns as they are in Philadelphia and some other big cities. Instead, gay clubs and their patrons spill out through wide-open French doors onto the Bourbon

Street sidewalks, right alongside straight establishments. Anyone can just wander in and out, drinks in hand. It makes for the most festive party atmosphere in the entire known gay universe. Y'all come.

BEST TIME TO COME

Anytime but summer.

GETTING INTO TOWN

The official **Airport Shuttle** (522-3500) drops you off at your hotel and costs $10 one-way, but they take up to 11 people per van so if your stop comes last it'll be a long ride. If there are two of you, take a cab ($21). The ride takes about 30 min.

GETTING AROUND

You won't need a car here. Public transport is decent, and the French Quarter, where you'll spend most of your time, is easily walkable.

STAY

The French Quarter Reservation Service (940 Royal St Suite 263, New Orleans 70116, 523-1246). Central clearing house for several gay-oriented B&B's.

GAY

Ursuline Guest House (708 Ursuline, 525-8509). The gayest hostelry in New Orleans (about 85%). The 14 rooms in this circa-1860 home and adjacent former slave quarters are on the small side, but the owner has furnished them with taste, and many face a quiet courtyard. Try to get room 1 if you can. Rates hover around the $80 range, depending on time of year and room type.

GAY-FRIENDLY

Although most of the following are gay-owned and/or operated, and advertise in the gay press, on any given day you could check in and find not a single gay person in residence.

Bourgoyne Guest House (839 Bourbon St, 525-3983). Offers two lugubrious suites and three small studios. Not an attractive place, and only about half gay. Dirty wall-to-wall carpeting and other signs of disrepair. But the price is right, the location good, and the owner friendly.

Rates: $57 (single), $60 (double) or $130 (four people in a suite).

Lafitte Guest House (1003 Bourbon St, 800-331-7971 or 581-2678). Prime Bourbon Street location, gracious management, and 14 antique-filled rooms—gets top marks in this category. Each room of this gay-owned and -operated 1849 manor house is different. On our visit, about 50% of the guests were gay, with older straight couples making up the rest. Includes continental breakfast and evening happy hour in the large sitting room; parking (a big plus) just $5 a night. Rates: $79-$165.

New Orleans Guest House (1118 Ursuline St, 566-1177). Just outside the French Quarter on a less-than-inviting street, with about 10% gay clientele, but rooms are cheery, clean, and tasteful. Rates: $59-$99.

Rober House (822 Ursuline, 529-4663). Really a condo development, but a tastefully-renovated, historic one. It's also the best buy in New Orleans. One charming Creole cottage sleeps up to six people. Units feature hardwood floors, a fully-equipped kitchen, separate dining and living rooms, laundry, and use of the attractive pool. Other accommodations are available. Rates: $69-$125.

47

BEST BEDS

If you have the money and don't need to stay gay, you'll find a warm welcome at any of these top-quality straight-oriented establishments. **The Windsor Court** (300 Gravier St, 800-262-2662, rates from around $195 to $350) is the best full-service hotel in town, especially if you're a repeat visitor. **Soniat House** (1113 Chartres St, 522-0570, regular rooms $135-$185, suites $225-$350) is a New Orleans gem. **The Melrose** (937 Esplanade Ave, 944-2255, $225-$375) resembles the elegant private home it once was and the owner makes guests feel right at home—top drawer in every way.

SEE/DO

TEN THINGS NO SELF RESPECTING GAY PERSON SHOULD MISS

Top of the Mart (2 Canal St, 33rd floor, 522-9795). Start with an orientation and a drink atop the World Trade Center, one of the largest revolving bars in the world, taking 90 minutes to make a full revolution. From up here, you understand how the Crescent City got its name. Just before sunset is the best time to watch ships ply the serpentine Mississippi and the city's twinkling lights go on one by one.

The Beauregard-Keyes House and Garden (1113 Chartres St, 523-7257). Tour this 1826 Greek Revival manse.

The Gallier House Museum (1118-1132 Royal St, 523-6722). Another historic house tour. James Gallier, the city's most famous architect, lived here.

The Garden District. Walk past block after block of elegant homes— Greek Revival, Victorian, Queen Anne, Second Empire, and other periods.

Nottoway Plantation (White Castle, LA, 545-2730). Rent a car and drive out to see this and the many historic plantations along the Mississippi River Road.

Audubon Zoo (6500 Magazine St, 861-2537). Come here via the river-boat *John James Audubon.* Departs daily from the Aquarium every two hours from 10 am to 4 pm.

48

St Charles Avenue Streetcar. Go for a ride on the world's oldest con-tinuously operating street railway (take it back from the Zoo to the French Quarter).

French Quarter. Simply meander along the streets. Even if you get lost you'll enjoy the experience.

The Friends of the Cabildo (523 St Ann St, 523-3939). Take one of their walking tours, offered twice daily.

The Presbytere (751 Chartres St, 568-6968). Artifacts showcasing the city's history.

SPECIAL EVENTS

Pridefest happens during Oct. But **Mardi Gras** (it can fall anytime between Feb 3 and Mar 9, depending on the year) is the main annual gay (and straight) event.

KEEP FIT/RECREATION

There is no well-equipped truly gay gym here. The reason is simple: this is New Orleans. People come here to smoke cigarettes, drink, and party, not pump their pecs.

The Club (515 Toulouse St, 581-2402). Closest thing within walking dis-tance of the French Quarter, a full-fledged bath house that includes a fairly well-equipped but cramped gym on first floor (free weights mostly). Upstairs exercise of a different nature takes place. No day fee: Six-month membership costs $50 and entitles you to four hours of gym use per day.

Elmwood Fitness Center at One Shell Square (701 Poydras, 13th Fl, 588-1600). Excellent equipment and aerobics, with a large number of gay members. Day fee: $10.

EAT

In New Orleans, people don't eat to live, they live to eat. There are so many wonderful restaurants that they're reason alone to visit. But there aren't any great all-gay restaurants and, in fact, very few predominantly gay ones, although many are gay owned and operated. A number of old-guard restaurants still attract a loyal following, places where jacket and tie are *de rigeur* and the menus haven't changed in years—**Arnaud's, Antoine's, and Gautreau's**, to name a few. But many locals say these places are living off their reputations, and now suffer from spotty service and other flaws. Gallatorie's is still worth visiting, however, and Fri afternoons are a ritual with locals and tourists alike: be prepared to stand in line for hours, since they don't take reservations.

49

GAY-FRIENDLY

Old Dog New Trick Café (307 Exchange Alley, 522-4569). Gay-owned, offers organic, exotic, New Orleans vegetarian cooking for lunch and dinner.

TOP TABLES

The Grill Room (Windsor Court Hotel, 300 Grozier St, 522-1992, entrees $27-$45) ranks as one of the city's best eateries; **Mike's on the Avenue** (628 St Charles Ave in the Lafayette Hotel, 523-1709, entrees $17-$24) features new-wave food like the flash-fried beer-battered Louisiana oysters with Mike's green chili sauce; **Bayona** (430 Dauphine St, 525-4455, entrees $13-$19) offers dishes such as grilled hoisin tuna with sesame guacamole and shellfish with spicy shrimp and carrot sauce.

PLAY/MEET

At last count, there were over 30 clubs and bars in New Orleans and the immediate suburbs, most of them open 24 hours a day. No matter what the caliber of the patrons, though, you'll find them noticeably more friendly than in other cities. You'll also find wilder action in New Orleans than almost anywhere else, especially during Mardi Gras and other special events. Everyone lets it all hang out—and I mean all, and I mean hang. I've omitted a number of smaller neighborhood and hustler bars.

MOSTLY FOR DRINKING/CRUISING

The Golden Lantern (1239 Royal St, 529-2860). Has been around for more than a quarter-century; the patrons have been around a long time, too.

Wolfendale's (834 N. Rampart St, 524-5749). Popular with people of color, features strippers and a DJ on weekends.

Café Lafitte in Exile (901 Bourbon St, 522-8397). Oldest bar in New Orleans, although the crowd isn't. Worth a stop on your pub crawl.

Mississippi River Bottom (515 St Philip St, 586-0644). Your typical neighborhood gay dive, with pool tables and such. Exotic dancers on weekends.

50

MOSTLY FOR DANCING

Oz (800 Bourbon St, 593-9491). Relative newcomer, spins the hottest tunes and stages some outrageous floor shows. Located on two levels with outdoor and indoor balconies, it attracts a young crowd with a smattering of straight kids who wander in off the street to see what all the excitement is about.

Bourbon Pub/Parade (801 Bourbon St, 529-2107). Bar with a separate disco (Parade) on the second floor. The outdoor balcony is a popular place to watch the gay world go by. The bar features several video monitors showing homoerotic clips. Youngish crowd.

LEATHER

The Phoenix (941 Elysian Fields Ave, 945-9264). Caters to the leather crowd. Bring-your-own-meat barbecues on the patio are a summer tradition. Upstairs is the **Men's Room**, reputedly a no-holds-barred sex club. Both are open until 5 am (not 24 hours).

FOR LESBIANS

Charlene's (940 Elysian Fields Ave, 945-9228). Across the street from The Phoenix, the most popular spot for ladies.

SHOP

New Orleans is an antique maven's paradise—in fact, with hundreds of one-of-a-kind stores, it's a shopper's heaven. Wander down Royal St to sample the antique offerings.

Accents (713 Royal St, 524-4587). Features unusual jewelry, carnival masks, frames, and paperweights.

Postmark New Orleans (631 Toulouse St, 529-2052). Gay-owned, a definite must-shop. These super-friendly transplanted Texans stock unusual cards, gifts, jewelry, homewares, and more.

The Riverwalk Marketplace (between Canal and Julia Sts, 522-1555). Encompasses over 200 shops and restaurants, including household names like Banana Republic and the Nature Company.

Robinson's Antiques (610 Toulouse St, 523-6683). Gay-owned, just one of many shops filled to the rafters with good, if expensive, stuff.

RESOURCES

51

GENERAL INFORMATION

Greater New Orleans Tourist and Convention Center (566-5011).

GAY/HIV INFORMATION

Lesbian and Gay Community Center of New Orleans (816 N. Rampart St, 522-1103). To get the latest dish, start your visit here.

NO/AIDS Task Force (1407 Decatur St, 945-4000). Largest AIDS group in the city.

BOOKSTORE

Faubourg Marigny Bookstore (600 Frenchmen St, 943-9875). New Orleans' gay and lesbian book source. Helpful and knowledgeable staff.

PUBLICATIONS

Ambush (PO Box 71291, New Orleans 70172, 522-8049). Bar rag.

Impact (511 Marigny St, 70152, 944-6722). More serious biweekly.

New Orleans This Week (866-6072). Sporadically-published pocket-sized guide to gay-oriented events, with some light editorial just for fun.

Southern Forum (PO Box 19529, New Orleans 70179, 523-2579). Monthly glossy magazine.

NEW YORK

WHAT TO EXPECT

The center of the known gay universe used to be in Greenwich Village, specifically the West Village, site of the Stonewall riots reputed to have given birth to the gay movement. The **Stonewall Inn** was a private club back then, when, in 1966, gay men anointed the corner of Christopher Street and Seventh Avenue as gay central. One night in the spring of 1969, the police raided the Stonewall, arresting everyone inside. After several nights of harassment, enough was enough, and the famous riots changed the course of gay history. But history keeps on changing. Now, Chelsea, especially West 17th between 5th and 8th Avenues and 8th Avenue between 17th and 19th Streets, ranks as New York's gayest neighborhood. Even A Different Light, the long-running gay bookstore, has moved here, further solidifying Chelsea's dominance. Gradually, the bars and clubs in the West Village—an area that some consider dangerous and over-run by Bridge and Tunnel people—have become passé.

New York's bar and club scene must be the most complex in the world. Just a few short years ago, in part as a response to AIDS, gay nightlife here was on the danger list. Now, thanks to an influx of younger gay men, the scene booms once again. Over 50 semi-permanent bars vie for your business in Manhattan alone. Besides the obvious mainstream choices, there are semi-hidden neighborhood places, underground sex clubs, private parties, after-hours hideouts, bars that cater strictly to minorities, and dozens of joints in the other boroughs. In addition, there are clubs within clubs—various promoters take over a disco for one night a week and "rename" it, such as "Crisco Disco at Crowbar". Most, but not all of these places are listed in Homo Xtra and Next, the two most popular bar/club rags (HX has the most complete listings). The clubs can be daunting: some are very large, all are noisy and smoky. Most feature go-go boys with ego-bruising bodies in various states of undress. You'll see drug use and even the kind of back-room groping that you thought went out years ago. Surprise. Clubs open late, and don't get busy until 1 am or so. With the aid of youthful vigor, disco naps, or dubious boosters like Ecstasy and other amphetamine-like drugs, the action continues until the morning light.

BEST TIME TO COME

Spring and fall are best. The weeks just before Christmas are also popular.

GETTING INTO THE CITY

Tel Aviv Car Service (800-222-9888) will whisk you to and from the airport in sedan comfort. From Newark Airport, take the **NJ Transit** bus to the **Port Authority Bus Terminal.**

GETTING AROUND

Subway (info: 718-330-1234) and taxis are best bets. You won't want or need a car.

STAY

GAY

The Colonial House (318 W. 22nd St, 243-9669). I know this is not the only gay guest house in NYC, but the it's only one I'd recommend. Twenty rooms, 8 with private baths, some with working fireplaces, on a tree-lined street. The roof deck affords enough privacy for au naturel sunning. Rates: $65-$80 shared bath, $99 private bath.

GAY-FRIENDLY

Really, you'll find any hotel in New York gay-friendly. Here are two of my favorites for those on a budget:

Paramount (235 W 46th St, 764-5500). Oh-so-cool hotel with bellhops chosen primarily for their looks; go and gawk. Small rooms with avant garde design. Rates: around $150 weekday, $100 weekends.

The Franklin (164 E 87th St, 369-1000). Upper East Side alternative to the Paramount, great location for museum hopping. A favorite—top value, includes parking and continental breakfast; stylish, newly-decorated rooms. Rates: around $130.

BEST BEDS

The Carlyle Hotel (Madison and 76th St, 744-1600). The only five-diamond (Mobil's highest rating) in New York. Also the closest thing to European service you'll find. The 400 staffers (for half that number of rooms) have been here for years if not decades, and will coddle you.

Corner rooms in the tower ending in "04" (3204, 3304) have rush-to-the-window, sensational views for $360 a night and are in high demand.

SEE/DO

TEN THINGS NO SELF-RESPECTING GAY PERSON SHOULD MISS

N.Y. Gay and Lesbian Community Center (208 W. 13th St, 620-7310). Good place to get oriented.

The Circle Line (W 42nd St at the Hudson River, 563-3200). Fun, useful river tour of Manhattan.

The Empire State Building (350 5th Ave, 736-3100). Great views.

55

The Frick Collection (1 E. 70th St, 288-0700). World-class museum with engrossing special exhibits.

The Guggenheim Museum (1071 5th Ave at E. 76th St, 423-3500). Frank Lloyd Wright designed this unusual space. Excellent permanent collection and special shows.

The Metropolitan Museum (5th Ave and 82nd, 535-7710). The foremost repository of art in the country.

Barney's Uptown (660 Madison Ave, 8326-8900). Sensational clothes, men.

Central Park (427-4040 for weekend tours). One of the great urban parks, much safer than press reports would have you believe, at least during the day.

Ellis Island (363-3200). Visit the actual arrival hall where so many immigrants (including my father) first arrived in the US.

Leslie Lohman Gay Art Foundation (131 Prince). Unique gallery showing works of gay and lesbian artists.

Modern dance at the Joyce Theater (175 8th Ave, 242-0800). One of the great cultural institutions of New York, frequented by gays.

KEEP FIT/RECREATION

New York has more gay-oriented gyms than any other city—in fact, *Next* (see under **Publications**) lists 20 gay-friendly or gay-owned fitness centers in the metro area.

American Fitness Center (128 8th Avenue, 627-0065). In the center of gay New York, this partially gay-owned gym is the biggest in town, with 10,000 sq. ft. of free weights. The cardiovascular section is upstairs. A large swimming pool is planned, pending landlord permission. Women are welcome, and tend to leaven the preponderance of super-hunky gay men. Day fee: $15.

Better Bodies (aka Bitter Beauties) **and Extreme Cardio** (22 W. 19th St, 969-6789). Diverse clientele, mostly men. Day fee: $8.

Chelsea Gym (267 W. 17th St, corner of Eighth Ave, 212-255-1150). The original New York gay fitness emporium. It became seedy and unpopular in the 1980s, but is now enjoying a revival. Still the cruisiest, steamiest gym in town, its no ladies policy enhancing the sexual tension. Day fee: $15.

David Barton Gym (552 6th Ave, 727-0004). Small, cruisy, with friendly staff. Day fee: $15.

SPECIAL EVENTS

The annual **Halloween Parade in Greenwich Village** attracts fantastically-clad revelers, gay and straight. The **Gay Pride Parade** is held every June.

EAT

Forty thousand restaurants call New York home, so choosing just a few is a highly subjective proposition. You needn't confine yourself to a gay restaurant, although there are many good ones with cute waiters and fun atmospheres. Here are some of my favorites, both very gay and not-so-gay.

TRES GAY

Cola's (148 8th Ave, 633-8020). Nicola Accardi owns this small storefront eatery and cooks up regional Italian cuisine with a healthy touch. You can't go wrong with any of the pastas and entrees, especially the rigatoni with portobelli and asparagus, and seared mahi mahi with black olives and capers. Entrees: $8-$11.

Eighteenth & Eighth (159 8th Ave, at 18th St, 242-5000). Small storefront eatery popular for breakfast, lunch, and dinner. Service is friendly, the food decent, and the price right. I liked the roast pork loin stuffed with herbs and spices and salmon with black olive sauce. Entrees: $9-$12.

Food Bar (149 8th Ave, 243-2020). Formerly Rogers and Barbero. With its hardwood floor and post modern design, now a popular gay hang with simple, low-cost main courses like spicy southern fried chicken with black eyed pea salad and soba noodles with vegetables. The waiters work their good looks to full advantage. Entrees: $6-$10.

Kiss Bar & Grill (142 W. 10th St, 242-6444). One of New York's newer gay restaurants, the small menu lists items like grilled marinated tuna with tarragon sauce and pineapple salsa. Tablecloths, and a room-length bar along one side. Most entrees under $12.

Manatus (340 Bleeker St, 989-7042). This 24-hour Village cheap eats mecca attracts a 50%-90% gay clientele depending on the night. Entrees: most around $10.

Universal Grill (44 Bedford St, 989-5621). Perhaps the gayest restaurant in the universe. Serves breakfast, lunch, and dinner to a lively, young crowd. Menu includes items like pecan-crusted chicken with plantain-ginger stuffing and penne with grilled tuna, tomatoes and calamata olives. Great place to celebrate a birthday (they make a fuss). Entrees: $11.50-$17.

The Viceroy (160 8th Ave, 633-8484). Nicola Accardi's latest restaurant is the largest in gay Chelsea. The nouvelle comfort food menu emphasizes low-fat ingredients like grains and vegetables. Entrees: $10-$19.

GAY FRIENDLY

Lucky Cheng's (24 First Ave, 473-0516). Chinese waiters in drag and a mixed gay/straight clientele do not necessarily a gay restaurant make. Straight yuppies and tourists have discovered this place with a vengeance. The food sounds better than it tastes: crispy soy chicken with pancakes and Asian apple salsa, steamed whole fish with ginger and a chili cilantro sauce. Entrees: $5-$13.50, with some specials higher.

TOP TABLES

Zagat's and other foodies consistently rank these places as the Big Apple's best restaurants:

Aureole (34 E. 61st St, 319-1660); **Bouley** (165 Duane, 608-3852); **44** (44 W. 44th St, 944-8844); **Union Square Cafe** (21 E. 16th St, 243-4020); **Le Bernardin** (155 W. 51st St, 489-1515); **Le Cirque** (in the Mayfair Hotel, 58 E. 65th St, 794-9292); **Lutece** (249 E. 50th, 752-2225).

PLAY/MEET

MOSTLY FOR DANCING

Okay, where do we begin. Describing the New York club scene is like trying to narrate the Benjamin Moore paint chip rack. Let's start our tour with the dance venues that get most of the attention as of the moment:

Bump! at Palladium (126 E. 14th bet 3rd and 4th Ave). Formerly at the now-defunct and more interesting Club USA. Mixed gay/straight on Fri, gay on Sun.

Limelight (47 W 20th St, 807-7850). Church-turned-disco. Even though this place was popular ten years ago and lots of tourists and straight people come here, it's still happening, especially on Wed and Fri nights. The **lick it! lounge**, a club within a club, encourages freedom of sexual expression.

1984 at The Crow Bar (339 E. 10th St, 420-0670). Voted best Bar 1992 and Best Small Club 1993 by *HX*, small and dark Crow Bar adopts a different persona every night. Every Fri, "1984" is one of those guises; the music is from, you guessed it, 1984 or thereabouts—pure nostalgia disco and tons of fun.

The Roxy (515 W 18th, 645-5156). Expensive admission and drinks, hot on Sat nights, closed on Fri and Sun. Best time to come: Thu, when **disco interruptus,** a disco oldies dance party, takes over and a discretionary door policy (shades of Studio 54—only the attractive may enter) is in effect.

Sound Factory Bar (12 W. 21st St, 206-7771). Another great place for dancing and video-watching (in the space that once housed Private Eyes). Packed most nights of the week. Not to be confused with the now-defunct Sound Factory.

Spectrum (802 64th St, Brooklyn, 718-238-8213). Not in Manhattan, but it's all-gay. Your chance to be a Bridge and Tunnel person in reverse. *Saturday Night Fever* filmed here, lots of John Travolta wannabes.

The Tunnel (220 12th Ave at 27th, 695-8238). Opens at midnight on Sat, which is the gayest night, and attracts a native Manhattan (as opposed to tourist or Bridge and Tunnel) crowd.

MOSTLY FOR DRINKING/CRUISING

The Break (232 8th Ave at 22nd, 627-0072). Sister bar to The Works.

Outdoor area gets busy on warm evenings. Jammed with locals when low-cost drink specials are on offer.

Champs (17 W. 19th St, 633-1717). Popular new "sports" bar with live DJs and go-gos. Giving Splash a run for its gym bunnies. $1 margaritas on Wed.

Splash (50 W. 17th St, 691-0073). The club everyone says they hate, but why are they always there? Stylish, located in the heart of gay Chelsea, popular with the after-work crowd.

The Townhouse (236 E. 58th St, 754-4649). Bills itself as an elegant hideaway but resembles a funeral parlor—okay, an elegant funeral parlor. Full of prissy queens with attitude, lots of suits and ties, and married men making a stop between the office and the 6:02.

59

Uncle Charlie's (56 Greenwich Ave, 255-8787). At one time this Greenwich Village spot could justly bill itself as New York's most happening spot, but no longer. Go-go boys on Fri, $1 beer specials Sun after 5 pm, plus 2-for-1's other nights 5-9 pm.

The Works (428 Columbus Ave, 799-7365). Popular, smallish, and friendly bar, one of the few located this far uptown.

LEATHER

The Lure (409 W 13th St, 741-3919). New York's serious leather bar. Enforced dress code.

The Spike (120 11th Ave at W. 19th, 243-9688). No longer strictly leather (the Lure seems to have upstaged it). Cruisy.

SEX PARTIES

At last count, there were over a dozen private sex clubs/parties available for the adventurous. Some are by invitation only or have a discretionary door policy (if you're not hot, you don't get in). Examples: **He's Gotta Have It** (135 W. 14 St, 677-3599), a bi-weekly sex club in a large loft space; **Afrodeeziak** (3 E. 128th St, Harlem, 996-2844), a check-your-clothes brownstone club mostly for Black and Latin men); and **Carter's New York Prime** (388-8043), a roving orgy that auditions newcomers during clothes-on hotel suite cocktail parties (they tell management they're having a bachelor party. Yeah, right). See *HX* for the most up-to-date listings. Offering the same kind of entertainment, several "dark rooms" vie with each other.

SHOP

All American Boy (131 Christopher St, 242-0078). Long-established source for male fashion.

Gay Pleasures (546 Hudson St, 255-5756). Rents and sells male erotica in an atmosphere reminiscent of a country store. The surroundings and staff make you feel at home rather than at the average 42nd Street smut shop—they actually greet you with "hello, can I help you find anything?"

The Loft (89 Christopher St, 691-2334). Mostly gay male clientele, latest in fashion forward.

P. Chanin (152 8th Ave, 924-5359). Chic Chelsea clothing, cards.

Rainbows & Triangles (192 8th Avenue, 627-2166). Sells all the usual cards, gifts, books, magazines, and haircuts.

RESOURCES

GENERAL INFORMATION

General New York info: 800-I-LOVE-NY.

Newcomer's Handbook™ for New York (First Books, 312-276-5911). Tremendously useful book for anyone (gay or straight) *moving* here.

GAY/HIV INFORMATION

Gay Men's Health Crisis (807-6655) for AIDS info.

BOOKSTORES

A Different Light (151 W 19th St, 989-4850). Emblematic of the "move" from the West Village to Chelsea, this long-time Village landmark has relocated. Outlets in San Francisco and West Hollywood. Mail order: 800-343-4002.

Creative Visions (548 Hudson, 645-0395). Occupies A Different Light's old digs; selection isn't as large as ADL's, but good stock of lesbian titles.

The Oscar Wilde Memorial Bookshop (15 Christopher St, 255-8097). Village institution since 1967.

PUBLICATIONS

Homo Xtra (19 W. 21st St, Suite 504, 10010, 627-5280). Bills itself as "the totally biased, politically incorrect party paper," and contains gossip, bar and club schedules (essential reading), unopinionated restaurant reviews, and scorching personal ads.

Next (227 E. 56th St, 10022, 832-7188). Resembles HX except it's a glossy four-color mini-mag.

Metrosource (622 Greenwich St, 10014, 691-5127). Combines a gay yellow pages with feature articles of unusually high quality.

New York Native (PO Box 1475, Church St Stn, 10008, 627-2120). The long-running tabloid of serious politics and issues, famous for its championing of unconventional AIDS wisdom, but also includes personals and arts/entertainment info.

LOS ANGELES

WHAT TO EXPECT

In order to understand LA, you have to understand Disneyland. LA is a series of theme parks, haphazardly arranged. After all, this is where the concept was invented. West Hollywood is a gay theme park. Beverly Hills is a shopping theme park, and so on. The other thing to remember about Los Angeles is that there is no such thing as gay Los Angeles. Rather, there are six or seven distinct gay communities that, were they in Minnesota or Colorado, would qualify as major homo hubs. The separate incorporated city of West Hollywood is what most people mean when they talk of gay LA. How gay is it? As Peter Theroux says in his book *Translating LA,* only the Vatican has a lower birth rate. And as my friend David says, "So many good-looking men it gives you a headache." Yet I was surprised one night to find carloads of heckling teenagers cruising down Santa Monica Boulevard, West Hollywood's main drag, making snide remarks to the men holding hands as they walked from club to club. That wouldn't happen in the Castro—the hecklers would be torn limb from limb.

But WeHo is only part of the story. Just over the border, Los Angeles proper maintains its own gay enclaves, such as Silverlake, a less pretentious district where gay men and women go to nest. Long Beach, Orange County, Santa Monica, North Hollywood, and Studio City are some of the other gay enclaves near LA. And 90 minutes to the south of West Hollywood, Laguna Beach is another gay mecca—a smaller, more upscale version of Provincetown, with a couple of gay bars and one gay hotel.

Many of the time-honored clichés about LA, you discover, are based in truth: the place is very horizontal. Everyone lives in severe denial about the smog—it's always "haze," or "fog;" it'll burn off. They lie about the length of their commute. And you really are what you drive. And everyone obsesses about their looks. Witness all the ads placed in the gay press for cosmetic surgery, tanning, fat removal, personal trainers, and teeth whitening (one placed by The Tooth Fairy, a gay dentist, who "likes them white and straight—your teeth, that is.") Why come here, what with the narcissism, the riots, the fires, the floods, the quakes, and all the rest? Well, precisely because everyone spends so much time on body beautiful, there's a lot of nice scenery. And between disasters, you'll benefit from good sightseeing of a different kind—the enlightening museums, fun theme parks, and world-class beaches. So whether you're just passing through, moving here, visiting friends, or looking for love, you'll enjoy yourself.

BEST TIME TO COME

Anytime except during an earthquake, flood, or riot.

GETTING INTO THE CITY

Take a van service like Super Shuttle, or drive.

GETTING AROUND

64

You definitely need a car. Budget rents exotic models like BMWs and Mercedes.

STAY

GAY

The San Vicente Inn (837 N. San Vicente Blvd, 310-854-6915). West Hollywood's only all-gay lodgings. Twelve comfortable and tasteful rooms, eight with private bath; three self-contained cottages. Pool and Jacuzzi. Rates: $59-$99.

GAY-FRIENDLY

Ramada West Hollywood (8585 Santa Monica Blvd, West Hollywood, 310-652-6400). An excellent place to stay while visiting LA. Attractive, stylish rooms in gray tones. Outdoor heated pool. Friendly staff. For an extra $6, you can use the gay gyms across the street. Rates: $95-$129.

The Montrose (900 Hammond St, West Hollywood, 800-776-0666/310-855-1115). Great rooftop pool, tennis court, and terrace, 110 rooms—all junior suites or larger, with fireplaces, some with kitchenettes. Clientele about 30% gay. Bottle of good Chardonnay, fruit basket, and bottled water greet all guests. Small workout room with good equipment. Corporate rate: $129 (special off-season and weekend rates also available).

BEST BEDS

The Hotel Bel-Air (701 Stone Canyon Rd, 310-472-1211). This is definitely one the coolest hotels in the country. Pink stucco oasis, privacy, working fireplaces, terraces, Jacuzzi's in some rooms. A great place to escape for the weekend, and gays and lesbians are as welcome as anyone else—just bring tons of cash.

SEE/DO

Who says there's nothing to do in LA? Gobs of world-class museums, star-watching, theme parks—you could spend weeks here and not see it all.

TEN THINGS NO SELF-RESPECTING GAY PERSON SHOULD MISS

The J. Paul Getty Museum (17985 Pacific Coast Hwy, 310-458-2003). Major art. Make a parking reservation in advance.

Universal Studios (100 Universal City Plaza, 818-508-9600). The Back to the Future ride is fun.

65

NBC Studios (3000 W. Alameda St, Burbank, 818-840-3537). Watch the taping of a TV program, such as "The Tonight Show". Ticket counter opens weekdays 8-4.

The Museum of Contemporary Art (250 Grand Ave, 213-626-6222). Impressive collection of American and European paintings and sculpture.

Mann's Chinese Theater (6925 Hollywood Blvd, 213-464-8111). Worth a stop. Compare your foot size with that of your favorite star's or see a movie here.

Norton Simon Museum (411 W. Colorado Blvd, Pasadena, 818-449-3730). Lots of Van Goghs, Manets, and Monets.

Huntington Library (1151 Oxford Rd, Pasadena, 818-405-2141). Home of Gainsborough's *Blue Boy* and a Gutenburg Bible, plus beautiful gardens.

LA County Museum of Art (5905 Wilshire Blvd, 213-857-6000). Another world-class art venue.

Laguna Beach. 90 minutes or so south of West Hollywood, this is a mini-Provincetown with a large gay population and a couple of bars. Stay at the **Surf & Sand,** dramatically situated on the beach.

Motion Picture Coordination Office (6922 Hollywood Blvd, room 602, 213-485-5324). Here you can buy or just examine today's movie "shoot sheet," listing the movies, TV shows, and music videos that will be shot today, and who's starring in them.

International Gay and Lesbian Archives (310-854-0271). Reputedly an interesting place. Call for hours (and good luck—I've never been able to get anything but an answering machine, and they never returned calls).

SPECIAL EVENT

Sunset Junction. Annual late August street fair in Silverlake (3600-4400 blocks of Sunset Blvd). Music, food, things to buy.

KEEP FIT/RECREATION

The Athletic Club (8560 Santa Monica Blvd, 310-659-6630). 21,000 sq. ft. of serious body work. Outdoor pool with palm trees that looks like it belongs at a Westin; suntanning, hair salon, travel agency. 100% gay men, many of them shirtless. Equipment is in good shape, too. Day fee: $15 ($40 per week).

Gold's (1016 N. Cole Ave, Hollywood, 213-462-7012). Noisy, big, well-equipped, 70%-80% gay, *tiny* locker room. Less cruisy than the West Hollywood gyms, but the men are just as awesome. Day fee: $8, free if you're a Gold's member elsewhere.

The Sports Connection (8612 Santa Monica Blvd, WH, 310-652-7440). Aka the Sports Erection. Unlike the Athletic Club, no day guests allowed so not useful for tourists. Multi-tiered, very complete facility.

Body Builders Gym (2516 Hyperion Ave, Silverlake, 213-668-0802). In LA's Silverlake section, friendly, 95% gay, but not as glitzy or well-equipped as West Hollywood's gyms. Say hi to articulate leather stud "D." Cannon (punctuation his, not mine) if he's working behind the counter. Day fee: $10.

EAT

TRES GAY

Gays make up the majority of the clientele at nearly any restaurant in and around the Santa Monica strip. The following is just a sample of what's available:

The Abbey (692 N. Robertson, 310-289-8410). Great music, mostly outdoor dining. Coffee, tea, desserts, breakfast, healthy and light menu with things like curried chicken salad. Everything under $8.

Basix Café (8333 Santa Monica Blvd., WH, 213-848-2460). Tex-Mex, specialty pizzas, in-house bakery with low-fat and sugar-free selections. Entrees: everything under $10.

Mark's (861 N. La Cienega Blvd, 310-652-5252). Large gay presence, handsome waiters, see-and-be-seen atmosphere, good food. Entrees: $10-$16.

The Power Bar (8578 Santa Monica Blvd, WH, 310-289-1125). Health food snack bar/nutrition center near the gyms and therefore filled with buff bodybuilder boys. Waiters sling heavy attitude. Everything under $7, including a $4.50 salad bar.

Faulkner's (8865 Santa Monica Blvd, WeHo, 310-289-9777). Gay-owned and 90% gay clientele. Patio dining. Ostrich in port wine and pepper sauce is a signature item at this French-American newcomer. Entrees: $7-$17.

GAY FRIENDLY

Atlas Bar and Grill (3760 Wilshire Blvd, LA, 213-380-8400). An eccentric, witty, glamorous, gay-owned restaurant with exciting food and super entertainment (including owner Steve Noriega's hilarious homemade videos)—and *no waiter attitude!* The city was building a subway line right in front for several years and somehow this unusual four-year-old managed to survive—a testament to what awaits inside. If it's on the menu, the ahi tuna with tart mango salsa is a must-eat. Entrees: $8-$18.

Off Vine (6263 Leyland Way, LA, 213-962-1900). *90210's* Jason Priestley sat down a few tables away with entourage (didn't recognize him, but my celebrity-hound friend did). About 30% gay, sometimes more. Cute, no-attitude waiters. Entrees: $11-$18.

TOP TABLES

You'll probably want to visit **Spago** (8301 Sunset Blvd, WH, 213-656-6388). Okay food, but not really worth the hassle unless you're a celeb— you'll be put in what they call Siberia, the back room. Opt instead for **David Slay's La Veranda** (225 S. Beverly Dr, Beverly Hills 310-274-7246), an under-rated, friendly spot where you'll also see the famous and totally groove on the fried spinach leaves. Zagat rates **Patina** (5955 Melrose Ave, 213-467-1108) No. 1 for food. The restaurant in the **Bel Air Hotel** (see **Stay**, above) is also excellent.

PLAY/MEET

There's a thriving underground club scene here that changes weekly. Study a copy of *Spunk* (see **Publications**, below), or ask a bartender. This book covers only the highlights in West Hollywood and LA proper; in addition, Long Beach supports nearly 20 gay bars. Lots of sex clubs, too—after all, you've got to do something with that tanned-buffed-waxed gym body.

MOSTLY FOR DANCING

Arena/Circus Disco (6655 Santa Monica Blvd, Hollywood, 213-462-1291). Arena draws a young, mixed/alternative crowd (including Generation Q). Very Latin on Sat nights. Two dance floors, lots of bars. Not gay every night—call ahead. Fri night gay at Circus.

Axis (652 N. La Peer, WH, 310-2659-0471). Large dance/video club with several bars, valet parking. Thu through Sun. Young, buffed crowd.

Probe (836 N. Highland, 213-461-8301). Survival of the buffest—what you get when you mix steroids with crystal meth. Large (Sat only) dance club full of the well-buffed—everyone takes their shirts off, so don't go unless you're physically and mentally ready. Gets started late and goes until mid-morning Sun (if you don't do drugs, get a good night's sleep and come here for breakfast). Cover: $20.

Temple (213-243-0911). Roving warehouse dance club every Sat night. Popular with club kids.

MOSTLY OR CRUISING/DRINKING

The following are all in West Hollywood:

Micky's (8857 Santa Monica Blvd, 310-657-1176). Small dance floor, but mostly a video cruise bar with the usual stand-and-models.

Motherlode (8944 Santa Monica Blvd, 310-659-9700). As friendly as it gets on the strip. Sun beer bust.

Rage (8911 Santa Monica Blvd, 310-550-8851). Right on the strip, video dance bar. Lots of stand-and-model attitude.

Revolver (8851 Santa Monica Blvd, 310-550-8851). Video bar popular with perfectly-tanned white boys.

MOSTLY FOR ASIAN MEN

Mugi (5221 Hollywood Blvd, Hollywood, 213-462-2039). Popular bar for Asian men and their admirers.

LEATHER

Gauntlet II (4219 Santa Monica Blvd, Silverlake, 213-669-9472). Bills itself as LA's premier leather bar—three bars, pool tables, videos, cruisy Levi/leather crowd.

Faultline (4216 Melrose, Silverlake, 213-660-0889). Serious leather bar: leather, uniforms, etc.

The Spike (7746 Santa Monica Blvd, 213-656-9343). Dark leather-and-Levis place popular on Fri nights.

69

LESBIAN

The Palms (8572 Santa Monica Blvd, WH, 310-652-6188).

SEX CLUBS

One source told me that LA has more sex clubs than any other city.

Nighthawk (1064 Myra Ave, Silverlake, 213-662-4726). Fairly typical of the genre.

Vortex (1090 Lillian Way, Hollywood, 213-465-0188). Advertises itself as a private men's club. Fri is "Big Boner Night"—patrons sporting 8 inches or more get in free. One wonders how they measure.

SHOP

All American Boy (8947 Santa Monica Blvd, WH, 310-271-5747). West Hollywood outpost of this upmarket men's clothing store. Lots of Speedos, fashion-forward items like skirts and sarongs.

Don't Panic (802 North San Vicente Blvd, WH, 800-45-PANIC). Witty T-shirts and other fashion statements.

The Word (8935 Santa Monica Blvd, WH, 310-276-5979). Small, centrally-located shop for cards, wrapping paper, lube, condoms.

Video Active (2522 Hyperion, Silverlake, 213-669-8544). A thinking person's video store.

RESOURCES

GENERAL INFORMATION

The LA Visitor Bureau (Hilton Hotel, 685 Figueroa St, 213-689-8822).

Newcomer's Handbook™ **for Los Angeles** (First Books, 312-276-5911). Tremendously useful book for anyone (gay or straight) *moving* here.

GAY INFORMATION

The LA Gay and Lesbian Community Services Center (1625 N. Schrader Blvd, 213-993-7400). Best time to call or visit is after 4 pm.

BOOKSTORE

70

A Different Light (8853 Santa Monica Blvd, WH, 310-854-6601). LA outpost of this mini-chain.

PUBLICATIONS

Edge **(213-962-6994).** A tabloid-sized magazine.

Frontiers (213-848-2222). LA-based, but covers the known gay universe.

The Lesbian News (310-392-8224). Covers the female angle.

Nightlife (The Total Community Magazine). Covers all of the gay communities in and around LA.

Yes (213-848-2220). Covers the gay entertainment scene.

PHILADELPHIA

AREA CODE 215

WHAT TO EXPECT

P hiladelphia was founded by Quaker William Penn in 1682. In the 18th century it was the second largest English-speaking city in the world. From 1774 to 1800, the city's history was inextricably linked to the nation's: it was here on July 4, 1776 that delegates from the 13 colonies adopted the Declaration of Independence and, eleven years later, shaped the U.S. Constitution. At one point it seemed that Philly would be the nation's premier city, but events conspired against it, and New York and Washington eclipsed it economically and politically.

This home of the soft pretzel and the hoagie has always been a favorite with comedians, beginning with W.C. Fields, who wrote for his own epitaph, "On the whole, I'd rather be in Philadelphia." The City of Brotherly Love is used to getting back-handed compliments.

And it's used to being the kind of place that residents, gay and straight alike, love to hate. You hear a lot of griping—about white flight, the local gay business community (poorly-organized), and the gay social scene (it's limited essentially to one club, because the town won't support more). So it's easy to find gay men here who, like Fields, would rather be, if not dead, then at least elsewhere. And indeed, because the city is so close to New York and Washington, many gay men go to one or the other for a gay entertainment fix. Philadelphia is the second largest city on the East Coast, but it has always lived in the shadow of its larger northern neighbor, a mere hour and ten minutes away by Metroliner.

Despite the city's problems, there's a lot to see and do here, and Philadelphia offers much to the gay visitor. History and literature buffs could easily spend several days exploring places like Independence Hall and Walt Whitman's stomping grounds. Architecture-hounds will love the Federalist and Victorian row houses in Center City, especially in the Society Hill section—home to many gay men. It's worth walking up and down the narrow streets to explore Philly's many hidden alleys, and culture mavens will enjoy the terrific museums in Philly itself and nearby. With seven of the country's top 50 restaurants (according to a recent travel magazine poll) you could come just to eat. Plus, there are many opportunities for day trips, including nearby New Hope (see chapter under **The Resorts**).

GETTING THERE

If you can, arrive in Philadelphia by train. The renovated 30th Street Amtrak Station looks terrific, a real temple from an age grander than our own; it makes for a regal entry to the city. If you arrive by air, you can still use 30th Street: an airport express train goes between the aerodrome and the station.

GETTING AROUND

Parking is difficult in Center City, and nearly everything is within walking distance, so a car isn't necessary. There is decent public transportation and rental cars are available at 30th St. Station.

72

BEST TIME TO GO

Try to schedule your visit in the early spring or in the fall: the summers can be brutally hot.

STAY

GAY

Gaskill House (312-314 Gaskill St, 413-2887). One of the nicest urban retreats (of any sexual orientation) I've seen. This tastefully-restored 1828 townhouse, well-located near South Street in the Society Hill area, offers three attractively-furnished rooms, all with private bath, working fireplace, TV, VCR, and phone. No pets or smoking. Rates: $100-$140.

Uncle's Upstairs Inn (1220 Locust St, 546-6660). Six rooms all with private bath. Traditional decor, queen size beds. Above Uncle's, a gay bar, where there's a popular Sun brunch. Rates: $75-$95.

BUDGET CHOICE

The Barclay Hotel (237 S. 18th St, 545-0300). Inexpensive place close to gay central. Some of its 235 rooms boast real antiques; public rooms are very old world. Breakfast included. Rates: $75 (weekends)-$89-$99 (corporate).

BEST BEDS

The Four Seasons Hotel (1 Logan Cir, 963-1500). Generally acknowledged as the best place to stay, although the 371 rooms aren't large. Try to get a Logan Circle view. Rates: $150-$265, depending on day of week and season. **The Ritz Carlton** (17th and Chestnut Sts, 563-1600), manages to be bustling and serene at the same time. For you muscle muffins, there's a very good fitness center. Rooms on the club floors come with enough free food and drink to fill you up for days. Rates: $149 (weekends)-$195 (corporate).

SEE/DO

TEN THINGS NO SELF-RESPECTING GAY PERSON SHOULD MISS

Independence National Historical Park (between Walnut and Arch and Second and Sixth Sts, 597-8974). Twenty buildings on 46 acres, will keep you busy for a full day. Philadelphia's most popular tourist attractions: Independence Hall, the Liberty Bell, Old City Hall, and a number of lesser-known but still interesting monuments.

73

Bassett's (Reading Terminal, 12th and Arch). At $1.50 a pop, this is arguably the world's best ice cream. The city has converted an historic old train shed, once filled with scurrying commuters and Amish farmers, into a new convention hall. Still worth the detour—and the calories.

Walt Whitman House (330 Mickle Blvd, Camden, New Jersey, 609-964-5383). Whitman lived in this restored building for the last 16 years of his life. Take the Riverbus across the Delaware ($4 round trip) from the waterfront to the Aquarium and walk three blocks from there.

Furness Building (the Fisher Fine Arts Building) at the University of Pennsylvania. One of the greatest architect's greatest buildings. While at Penn, also check out alumnus Louis I. Kahn's ground-breaking **Richards Medical Research Building** (37th St and Hamilton Walk).

Gravers Lane Railroad Station (Gravers Ln and Anderson St, Chestnut Hill) . One of the cutest railroad stations anywhere. Honest.

Philadelphia Museum of Art (N. 26th St and Ben Franklin Prkwy, 763-8100). First-rate collection of works by Cassatt, Eakins, and the French Impressionists.

The Barnes Foundation in Merion (300 N. Latches Ln, 667-0290). Call for hours and visiting policy.

The Delaware Museum of Fine Arts (Kentmere Pkwy, Wilmington, 302-571-9590). Although often overlooked it houses a great collection of pre-Raphaelite paintings and is a short drive or train ride from Center City.

Brandywine River Museum (U.S. 1, Chadds Ford, PA, 388-2700). Full of Wyeths.

Rosenbach Museum and Library (2010 Delancey Pl, 732-1600). Rare manuscripts (like James Joyce's *Ulysses*); plus touring this Victorian mansion will give you a glimpse into how people lived back when people really lived. Former home of the two Rosenbach brothers, one of whom was a major clothes horse and never married. Hmmm.

KEEP FIT/RECREATION

Twelfth Street Gym (204 S. 12th St, 985-4092). Despite Philadelphia's size, at this writing there is no gay owned or operated gym in the city. This rabbit-warren of a place is the closest thing. Swimming, squash and racquet ball, basketball, electric beach, and aerobics; the weight and CV equipment here could use some updating and expansion. Day fee: $10.

SPECIAL EVENTS

PrideFest (not to be confused with the city's gay pride march) comes around each year in mid-May and is a good time to plan your visit. A big pier party and cookout are highlights. Call 800-767-FEST for information.

EAT

Philadelphia is a premier restaurant town—reason enough to come visit. What's unusual here is the large number of *gay* bar/restaurants with decent food.

TRES GAY

Judy's (Bainbridge and 3rd, 928-1968). Always packed with lots of gays and lesbians (80%-90% most nights), in part because every time you eat here they give you a two-for-one dinner entree coupon good for your next visit. With that, and a no reservation policy, the line often stretches out the door. Food, although not cutting edge, is satisfying, with entrees like pan fried rainbow trout in caper sauce and pasta primavera in sage cream sauce. Entrees: $11-$17.

Inn Philadelphia (251 S. Camac St, 732-2239). Gay-owned romantic fine dining restaurant with a large gay clientele. Choose between the pleasant garden or one of three fireplaced dining rooms on the second floor. Start with a cocktail in the bar on the first floor. Entrees: $14.50-$25.

Rodz (Rodman and 15th, 735-2900). Restaurant/cabaret/bar in an area just south of genteel Center City. Local jokesters, while praising the food, emphasize that it's Rod with a "z"—and indeed, when I visited on a Wed night, Rodz was just not happening. Tyz, the adjacent nightclub, was closed. A grand total of two gay couples were dining, and a handful more people were getting obliterated at the bar. Meat-oriented menu, steak and boneless breast of chicken and so on; Maryland crab cakes are a specialty when in season. Entrees: $9-$15.

The Westbury (13th and Spruce Sts, 546-5170). I heard good things about this neighborhood bar, but not such good things about **Venture** (a.k.a. Denture) **Inn** (255 S. Camac, 545-8731), an old standby bar/restaurant.

GAY-FRIENDLY

Astral Plane (1708 Lombard, 546-6230). Seafood fra diablo is a specialty on the seasonally-changing menu. Clientele of this partially gay-owned, nouvelle American holdout is only about 30% gay. Entrees: $9-$17.

75

CHEAP EATS

Millennium Coffee (212 S. 12th St, 731-9798). Happening gay coffee house—a great place to start your visit. Owners David Salkin and David Rumsey serve a variety of coffees and teas, along with sandwiches and sweets.

TOP TABLES

Le Bec Fin (1523 Walnut St, 567-1000, prix fixe $90, or lunch at $34) is reputedly one of best restaurants in the known universe (indeed, *Condé Nast Traveler* says it's *the* best restaurant in the US); **Circa** (1518 Walnut St, 545-6800, entrées $14-$18) is a restaurant, bar, and nightspot, all in a former bank building, with an eclectic crowd; **The Dining Room** (Ritz Carlton Hotel, 17th and Chestnut Sts, 563-1600, prix fixe $47) offers interesting fusion cuisine, wide-spaced tables, impeccable service; **The Fountain** (in the Four Seasons Hotel, 1 Logan Sq, 963-1500, tasting menu $59, entrees around $30) came in a close second after Le Bec Fin with Condé Nast Traveler readers, and is less expensive.

PLAY/MEET

"I went to Philadelphia," W.C. Fields joked about his native city. "It was closed." You hear different explanations, but the fact remains that old W.C. was on to something: Philadelphia's gay party scene is a yawn. Although the semi-official listing put out by *Philadelphia Gay News* includes around 20 bars and clubs (and even that's a surprisingly small number for what is supposedly the country's fourth largest city) in fact most people go to a place called Woody's, and the other joints just aren't happening, especially not during the week. Most people you talk to about the other bars have never heard of them, or they have something derogatory to say. Basically, Woody's is it.

MOSTLY FOR DANCING

Woody's (202 S. 13th St, 545-1893). You'll hear again and again, this multi-level Center City club is the only truly happening place in Philadelphia. Downstairs, a small café serves a limited menu, and a video bar attracts a slightly older crowd. Another bar (this one a base for younger men) awaits upstairs, as does a fairly large disco done up in Greco-Roman motifs. On Wed nights they let the under-21 crowd into the disco through a separate, unmarked entrance.

Key West (207 S. Juniper St, 545-1578). Smaller dance bar with theme nights and a brunch every Sun from noon to four.

76

MOSTLY FOR CRUISING/DRINKING

The 247 Bar (247 S. 17th St, 545-9779). Trying to be the naughtiest bar in town. During my visit, they got raided for showing porn films. This is Philadelphia, after all. Open mostly on weekends, male dancers.

The Two-Four Club (204 S. Camac St, 731-4377). After hours place where everyone goes when Woody's closes at 2 am. Trouble is, the Two-Four closes at 3 am, so you pay a pretty hefty cover for just an hour.

PIANO BARS

Raffles (243 S. Camac St, 545-6969). Piano bar with C&W dancing (call for details).

Rodz (1418 Rodman St, 546-1900, see under Eat). Small restaurant/bar with some decent entertainment.

FOR LESBIANS

Hepburn's (254 S. 12th St, 545-8088). The women's dance bar.

LEATHER

The Bike Stop (206 S. Quince St, 627-1662). Local leather & Levis hang. Dress code not strictly enforced.

SHOP

There isn't much happening here in the way of gay retail, other than the bookstores mentioned under **Resources**, below.

One Way (206 S. 13th St, 546-5944). Mainly clothing, with all the usual alluring underwear brands, some cards and books.

The 70 shops at **Liberty Place** (S. 17th and Market) include food outlets, craft stalls, and both one-of-a-kind and chain retailers. **Celebrate America: The Philadelphia Store** (567-1976) is a good place for souvenir hounds. **Coach, Benetton, J. Crew,** and their ilk are represented.

Many one-of-a-kind shops occupy the **South Street** area, and no visit to Philly is complete without a stroll down this sassy thoroughfare.

RESOURCES

GENERAL INFORMATION

Philadelphia Convention and Visitors Bureau: 636-3300.

GAY/HIV INFORMATION

Penguin Place (201 S. Camac, 732-2220). The gay and lesbian community center with especially worthwhile library and archives.

AIDS Information Network (922-5120).

AIDS Task Force of Philadelphia (545-8686).

BOOKSTORES

Afterwords (218 S. 12th St, 735-2393). Gay-owned; carries a thoughtful selection of gay books and publications (along with T-shirts, posters, and other items), but isn't exclusively gay.

Giovanni's Room (12th and Pine Sts, 923-2960). One of the best and largest gay/lesbian bookstores in the country, with an especially strong collection of imported books. The owner is knowledgeable about books and Philadelphia. Their authors series features readings by prominent gay and lesbian writers.

PUBLICATIONS

Au Courant (PO Box 42741 Philadelphia, PA 19101, 790-1179). The smaller, but livelier, competition.

Philadelphia Gay News (254 S. 11th St, 19107, 625-8501). One of the country's best gay publications.

SAN FRANCISCO

AREA CODE 415

WHAT TO EXPECT

So many gay men! Men kissing in the aisles of the Safeway—on the lips, for a long time. Men hugging on the subways and buses, holding hands in the cafes and restaurants. Gays kiss—and live—everywhere in the city by the bay. San Francisco's "minor" gay areas would be considered major gay neighborhoods were they located in any other metropolis. But the major area is, as everyone knows, the Castro. Here you'll feel no discomfort at all holding your lover's hand as you stroll past the interesting clothing stores whose windows are imaginatively decorated with the latest trendy duds. There are gay travel agencies, gay restaurants, gay bookstores, gay card shops.

The area south of Market Street has developed into an important neighborhood for clubs and restaurants. Every year the Folsom St Fair takes place in this bustling neighborhood, with its warehouses, studios, galleries, and night spots. Straights frequent South of Market (SoMa, as it's called), so some people may want to be a bit more circumspect here than in the Castro. And at night, it doesn't feel as safe as the Castro.

Writing about San Francisco is a bit daunting, but not because of all the public display of affection. This is gay central USA, after all, and it's hard getting a grasp on it. Something you should know right away: it's estimated that 50% of gay men here carry the HIV virus, and the rate of new infection among younger gay men is not going down. Yet it's still a vibrant place to visit and to live. San Francisco is small enough to be cliquish, but it's diverse—racially, sexually, and culturally—compared to cities like Boston or Philly. Asked how San Francisco is different from LA, the northern tribe will tell you that Southern California is conservative, another country. San Francisco enjoys cleaner air, better food, lovelier views. Her people are articulate, liberal, and can be as wacky as they like. Most people say that the American city that San Francisco most resembles is Boston. But unlike in Boston, people here don't care what you do—they don't judge. You can be a lesbian one day, bi the next, and heterosexual and married a week later and no one bats an eyelash. By the way, they don't call San Francisco "Fog City" for nothing. The mist floats in nearly every day like in an Andrew Lloyd Webber musical. Bring a sweater, even in summer.

BEST TIME TO COME

Anytime is fine. But summer weather is colder than you might imagine—in the 50's or 60's at times.

GETTING INTO THE CITY

Take a van service like Super Shuttle or drive.

GETTING AROUND

The SuperShuttle is the cheapest way in from the airport. The Muni (public transit) is convenient and safe (a one-day pass costs $6). BART is the faster rail system that links outlying areas with downtown. If you drive, make sure you park snugly against the curb, turning your front tire against it, and set the emergency brake or you'll get a ticket. Trust me.

STAY

As you might expect, the city offers a choice of gay-owned and mostly gay-clienteled B&B's.

GAY

Dolores Park Inn (3641 Dolores Pk, 621-0482). A former Pan Am flight attendant named Bernie owns this 1874 Italianate Victorian full of birds and dogs. One room features blue velvet drapes and a four-poster bed. Smoking is not allowed; all rooms have TVs, but only one comes with private bath. Full breakfast and afternoon wine is included. Rates: $60 single, $90 double; an extra luxurious private-bathed suite that sleeps four costs $165.

Inn on Castro (321 Castro St, 861-0321). Perhaps the most upscale option. Five rooms furnished in modern eclectic, all with private baths, in a convenient location. Good original artwork, cozy living room with fireplace, and a tasty full breakfast are just some of the charms you'll find in this restored Edwardian home. Rates: $75-$135.

24 Henry Street (24 Henry St, between Noe & Sanchez, 864-5686). The clientele of this 1880's home, with its five sunny and bright rooms (some with private bath), is almost entirely gay. Oriental rugs on wood floors in the homey front and rear parlors, friendly owners and atmosphere. Rates: $45-$85. Also available: a one BR apartment with VCR, microwave, and private phone for $95 a day.

Willows (710 14th St, 431-4770). None of the 11 sunny rooms here have private baths, but the Laura Ashley-esque fabrics are attractive, even if the willow furniture (hence the name) is not. Separate showers and WCs help prevent queues. Other nice touches: Direct dial phones in rooms (although calls can't be received after 10 pm), a convenient location, breakfast served in bed and nightly turn-down service with a glass of sherry. Lots of Euros and Aussies among the 99% gay male clientele. Rates: $74-$105 double, $66-$84 single, depending on room type, with lower prices during slower periods.

BUDGET CHOICE

Pensione (1668 Market St, 864-1271). Not gay-owned, but quite gay-friendly. Thirty-six well-maintained, small, and bright rooms with sinks but no private baths. Direct dial phones but no TVs. Inviting common areas with wingback chairs on each floor. Substantial European clientele, 75%-80% gay, 2 WC's and 2 baths per floor. 15 minute walk to either downtown or the Castro. Rates: $42-$58 depending on season.

81

BEST BEDS

Those not needing to stay in gay-owned establishments (and with deep pockets) should consider the **Mandarin Oriental** (222 Sansome St, 885-0999 or 800-622-0404) with stunning views of the bay and bridges from all guest rooms, and **Campton Place** (340 Stockton St, 781-5555 or 800-647-4007) a small boutique hotel with a noted restaurant, off Union Square. Both offer considerably discounted weekend rates.

SEE/DO

TEN THINGS NO SELF-RESPECTING GAY PERSON SHOULD MISS

Josie's Juice Joint and Cabaret (3583 16th St at Market, 861-7933). Great performance space for gay comics, singers, one-man and -woman shows.

Cafe Flore (corner of Noe & Market Sts, 621-8579). Wine, coffee, teas, pastries, lots of men—handsome and hip—lolling about looking intellectual and revolutionary (to the barricades, comrades, but first a double latte!) amid the terrace's verdant foliage.

Center for the Arts/Yerba Buena Gardens (701 Mission St, 978-2710). Interesting, new building south of Market.

Castro Theater (429 Castro St at Market, 621-6120). Lots of classic, campy films, complete with audience participation.

Cable car ride. If there's a line waiting to get on at the beginning of the route, it's sometimes easier to board a few blocks up.

Beach Blanket Babylon (Club Fugazi, 678 Green St, 421-4222). Long-running, super-campy musical revue with lots of gay men in the cast, but mixed gay/straight audience. Touristy, but fun.

Alcatraz (from Fisherman's Wharf, Pier 41, Red & White Fleet, 546-2700). The famous island prison. Advance tickets strongly recommended, as is the audio tour.

Wok Wiz (750 Kearny St, 355-9657). Walk through Chinatown with Food, folklore, history, led by local TV chef and cookbook author Shirley Fong-Torres or her assistants.

Cruisin' the Castro (375 Lexington St, 550-8110). Walking tour led by longtime resident Trevor Hailey. Reservations required.

Sausalito Ferry (Red & White Fleet, Pier 41, Fisherman's Wharf). For the view and shopping/strolling.

KEEP FIT/RECREATION

Market St Gym (2301 Market St, 626-4488). Medium-sized, almost all-gay but women allowed. Lots of free weights, spa, no steam room or aerobics. Bright, clean, newer equipment than Muscle Systems. Fairly cruisy. Day fee: $8.

Muscle Systems (2275 Market at 16th, 863-4700). The other main Castro gym, a.k.a. Muscle Sisters. Equipment less well-maintained than Market St Gym. No women permitted, very cruisy, high sexual tension. Also a branch at 364 Hayes St, 863-4701. Day fee: $8.

World Gym (260 DeHaro St at 16th, 703-9650). Large, serious body-building gym with 2000 sq ft aerobics floor. Mixed gay/straight, male/female. Day fee: $10.

EAT

Just about every restaurant in the Castro is tres gay; just about every restaurant in San Francisco is gay friendly.

TRES GAY

Anchor Oyster Bar (579 Castro St, 431-3990). Old standby small store-front restaurant with counter service. Mostly gay clientele. Crabcakes, shellfish platter, seafood pastas are specialties. Entrees: $9-$15.

Hamburger Mary's (1582 Folsom St at 12th, 626-1985). Popular South of Market spot with excellent tofu veggie burgers and dinner specials like chicken teriyaki. Entrees: $8-$10.

Carta (1772 Market St, 863-3516). Upscale storefront with international eclectic menu. Entrees: $10-$16.

Ma Tante Sumi (4243 18th St, 626-SUMI). Japanese/French cuisine in the Castro; gets mostly positive reviews; 80% gay. Menu, which includes popular fish and duck specials, changes seasonally. Entrees: $12-$16.50.

83

La Mediterranee (288 Noe St, 431-7210). This Lebanese-owned eatery serves up what is arguably the best food in the Castro at the most reasonable prices. Middle Eastern plate is the most popular dish. Entrees: $7-$8.

Pozole (2337 Market St at Noe, 626-2666). Big buff waiters with muscles for days—how do they get these gorgeous, friendly hunks to wait tables here? Entrees: under $8.

TOP TABLES

So many good restaurants, so little space and time. Try gay-owned **Zuni** (1658 Market St, 552-2522, $14-$18) for its pleasant interior of copper, wood, lots of glass, halogen lights, and steal beams as well as crowd-pleasing country French and Italian cuisine; another favorite is the **Cypress Club** (500 Jackson St, 296-8555, entrees $20-$25), a stylish spot with wild Hollywood musical decor, innovative fusion food, and a mostly straight expense-account clientele.

PLAY/MEET

The thing to remember is that there are nearly 100 places for gay people to dance and drink in this town, spread across three main geographical areas—the Castro, South of Market, and Polk St/Tenderloin. The selection is mind-boggling. If you really want to learn all about every possible bar and club, read *Betty & Pansy's Severe Queer Review*, available in most gay bookstores, which goes into hilarious detail about them all. In the words of Betty himself, "The club scene is a night-mare—a lot of one-night places that come and go, and are pretty much all the same." Suffice it to say, there's something for everyone. Note that most of the dance clubs are in the area called South of Market (aka SoMa). Savvy locals advise that you take a cab back and forth, since parking regulations are strict and enforced and there are many dark nooks and crannies along the way.

MOSTLY FOR DANCING

The Box (715 Harrison at 3rd, 647-8258). In a space called the Kennel Club. Serious dance club, racially mixed, with high-energy music. Thu nights only.

The End Up (401 6th St at Harrison, 496-9550). SoMa club made famous by *Tales of the City* (this is where Mouse does his strip act) with different clubs-within-a-club every night. Some parties begin at 6 am on weekends, including the Sun tea dance which has been going strong for over 20 years, but the other clublets change from month to month. Call 543-7700 for current configurations.

Pleasuredome (177 Townsend at 3rd, 974-1156). Sun night/Mon morning place for house, tech, and other new wave music. Young men on drugs.

FOR THE UPSCALE CROWD

Alta Plaza (2301 Filmore St, 922-1444). A.k.a. Ultra Plastic. Preten-tious polo shirt/sweater devotees frequent this pleasant, upscale bar.

The Lion Pub (2062 Divisadero at Sacramento, 567-6565). This place for men with real jobs also attracts the sweater crowd. Busy after work and after 8:30 pm. Not particularly cruisy—the kind of place you can bring your mother.

MOSTLY FOR CRUISING/DRINKING

Detour (2348 Market St between Noe and Castro, 861-6053). Hard-core cruise bar, busy every night mostly with guys in their 20's and 30's. Kind of grungy and punkish.

Midnight Sun (4067 18th St at Castro, 861-4186). Castro video bar standby with young preppy crowd.

Phoenix (482 Castro St at 18th St, 552-6827). Young, seemingly underage crowd—interracial and hip. Mostly a cruise bar, although its small floor is the only place to dance in Castro; busiest on weekend nights.

Q.T. II (1312 Polk at Bush, 885-1114). Typical of the Polk St area stripper and hooker bars, with live bands some nights. Best time to come: Fri and Sat nights or whenever they have strippers.

FOR NON-DRINKERS

Castro Country Club (4058 18th St at Hartford, 552-6102). Clean and sober space with good music, outside space with chaises, and TV theater. Weekends are busiest.

AFRICAN-AMERICAN/LATINO BARS

The Pendulum (4146 18th St at Collingwood, 863-4441). Super cruisy; strictly a scene for black guys—or white guys into black guys.

LESBIAN

The Café (2367 Market St at Castro, 861-3846). Balcony overlooking street, two bars, not exclusively women.

LEATHER

The Eagle (398 12th Street, corner of Harrison, South of Market district, 626-0880). Not exactly rough, but it is the city's premier leather bar. You won't be threatened here, and no one will look twice if you're not dressed head to toe in black cowhide—denim is also okay. Large outdoor space with an open fireplace, and special events, including a weekly Sun pm beer bust. A shop sells leather items.

Hole in the Wall (289 8th, 431-HOWL). Rowdy, up-and-coming, "biker" bar. Not for poseurs.

Lonestar (1354 Harrison at 10th, 863-9999). Full of bears—big and hairy, no aftershave-doused pretty boys need apply. There's outside space here, too.

SEX CLUBS

Blow Buddies (933 Harrison bet. 5th and 6th Sts, 863-HEAD). Just one of many in the city (**Eros** and **The Black House** are two others of note). Lots of mazes and non-locking booths with peepholes.

SHOP

San Francisco has more top-drawer men's clothing shops than any city in the US, with the possible exception of New York. It makes sense: lots of men, lots of clothes consciousness. The Castro is full of interesting gay-owned and -oriented shopping. The following is just a sampling.

Body (4071 18th St, 861-6111). Champion logo items, swimwear, hats, etc.

Does Your Mother Know (4079 18th St, 864-3160). Cards, wrapping paper, gifts. Neil is the friendly owner.

Main Line (516 Castro, 863-7811). Novelties for the home from around the world—unusual frames, clocks, cards, gifts, jewelry, shower curtains, candles, etc.

Rolo (2351 Market St, 431-4545). Dressiest clothing store in the Castro—everything Ralph and Calvin, including $30 T-shirts; some nice Italian imports.

Rolo Basics (450 Castro, 626-7171). Less expensive version of above. Utilitarian socks, T's, Rolo logo items, blue collar clothes.

Undercover (535 Castro St, 864-0505). Body-conscious activewear and swimwear.

RESOURCES

GENERAL INFORMATION

SF Visitor Bureau (Box 429097, San Francisco CA 94142; 391-2000).

GAY/HIV INFORMATION

STOP AIDS Project (201 Sanchez St at Market, 621-7177).

BOOKSTORE

A Different Light Bookstore (489 Castro St, 431-0891). One of three in the US (the others are in New York and LA). Great selection, helpful staff (especially Betty—his real name is John—of Betty and Pansy's "Severe Queer" Reviews).

PUBLICATIONS

The Bay Area Reporter is the largest and best gay weekly.

The Sentinel is a useful weekly.

Odyssey is more of a bar/sex rag with the best listings, and personals that sound like they were all written by the same person.

On-Q (243-4304). Relatively new, great maps and practical info.

WASHINGTON, D.C.

AREA CODE 202

WHAT TO EXPECT

For a gay person Washington offers all modern conveniences: good nightlife, great housing stock, lots of culture, a good gay bookstore, and relatively mild weather. The District also passed a comprehensive gay rights ordinance fairly early on. Sure, the summers are hot, racial tensions can get even hotter, and people shoot each other a lot. But most of the crime goes on in a few areas where tourists never venture. And Washington's tourist attractions are hard to beat—great museums, monuments, restaurants, shopping, architecture, entertainment.

Washington's gay history is interesting, to say the least. According to the owner of Lambda Rising, Washington's gay and lesbian bookstore, it's amusing to tour around D.C. looking for hidden signs of gay history: a statue of Alexander Hamilton holding hands with his male lover, and, in the Congressional Cemetery, J. Edgar Hoover's grave right next to that of Clyde Tolson, rumored to have been Hoover's favorite secret agent. And don't miss gay veteran Leonard Matlovich's tombstone with its epitaph, "They gave me a medal for killing a man, and discharged me for loving one."

According to many Washingtonians who have lived elsewhere, Washington is the country's most gay-comfortable city. Although Dupont Circle is still the center of the action, gays live everywhere. There are pockets in the suburbs in Northern Virginia, the Old Town section of Alexandria, and in places like Cheverly, Maryland, where same sex couples reportedly put an ad in the local paper thanking the citizenry for being such nice neighbors. (The nationwide trend is that more gays and lesbians are nesting in the suburbs, and Washington is no exception). Politicians support the community, and the climate of tolerance is improving. True, horrid people like Jesse Helms live here and give the city a negative image, but the District politicians are cool.

BEST TIME TO COME

Any time but summer; the Cherry Blossom Festival, centered around the blooming of Washington's many cherry trees, occurs in late March or early April.

GETTING INTO THE CITY

From the airport, take a cab or the clean, efficient Metro system.

GETTING AROUND

You won't need a car here, unless you take day trips out of town. The Metro system is one of the world's best—a marvel of technology and design, a tourist attraction in itself (this is what an urban subway system would look like if Walt Disney designed and ran it).

STAY

GAY

The Brenton (1708 16th St, NW, 332-5550 or 800-673-9042). Attracts a 99% gay or lesbian clientele. The high-ceilinged, public rooms boast hardwood floors and become a convivial gathering spot during the complimentary happy hours. Large and well-furnished rooms with oriental rugs and antiques (room 1 has a cozy sleigh bed). Ideal location short walk from Dupont Circle. No private baths, but a high ratio of baths to rooms. Rates: $69-$79 depending on whether single or double.

Capitol Hill Guest House (101 Fifth St, NE, 547-1050). Ten-room home (no private baths) far from the center of anything else gay. On the plus side: quiet parlor with ornately-carved mantel and hardwood floors, central air, and wooden shutters in the quiet rooms. Gay-owned and operated, attracts a mixed gay/straight crowd. Rates: $45-$80.

GAY-FRIENDLY

Kalorama Guest House (1854 Mintwood Pl, NW, 667-6369). The owner of this 31-room establishment, consisting of three separate houses, is straight (he's a novelist/psychiatrist who hangs with the likes of Stephen King and Tom Clancy). But the clientele can range from a high of 50% gay down to 0% on any given day. Stay here anyway for the doilies pinned on over-stuffed chairs, lace curtains blowing in the window, hardwood floors. Type of place where a gay motorcycle gang and a straight wedding party can share the property on a given weekend and everyone clicks. Super-pleasant gay manager. Rates: $45-$105.

The Radisson Barcelo Hotel (2121 "P" St, NW, 293-3100; 800-333-3333). Recommendable mainly because of its location. Rooms (300 of them) in need of refurbishment (nicked furniture, cigarette burns on the rugs); and a front desk in need of some attitude adjustment. Ask the reservations number to hunt for the lowest promotional weekend rates. Rates: as low as $90 weekends, beginning at $125 other times.

BEST BEDS

If you have the money and don't need to stay gay, Washington offers some of the best hotels anywhere. Among our picks:

ANA (2401 M St, NW, 429-2400) with its excellent fitness center frequented by gay men; **Four Seasons** (2800 Pennsylvania Ave, NW, 342-0444), probably the best full-service hotel in town; the **Morrison-Clark Inn** (Mass. Ave and 11th St, NW, 898-1200), elegant urban retreat with 54 rooms and suites; and **The Hay-Adams Hotel** (800 16th St, NW, 638-6600), where some of the 140 rooms, done in Edwardian and Georgian motifs, overlook the White House.

SEE/DO

Washington offers tons of fun to the gay visitor—world-class museums, historical sites, parks. Some of the best attractions lie just outside the city: Mt. Vernon and Monticello are two must-sees. You'll want to tour the **Capitol,** the **White House** (your Congressman can get you tickets—that's what they're there for), and see all the monuments, especially the **Vietnam Memorial** and the **Washington Monument**. Really, there's so much to do here that it's a bit futile listing a few personal favorites.

TEN THINGS NO SELF-RESPECTING GAY PERSON SHOULD MISS

The Holocaust Museum (100 Raoul Wahlenberg Pl between Independence Ave and D St, SW, 488-0400). The building is as impressive as what's inside. Chronicles the plight of European Jews, as well as homosexuals and other "undesirables." Bring tissues.

The Phillips Collection (1600 21st St, NW, 387-2151). Founded by collector Duncan Phillips, this neo-Georgian house exhibits an impressive array of modern art, including Renoir's *Luncheon of the Boating Party*.

The National Gallery of Art (Constitution Ave and 8th St, NW, 737-4215). This major league museum ranks among the best in the world. There's a little bit of everything, and a lot of some things, including important Impressionist works.

Monticello (Rte 20 and I-64, exit 121A, 804-295-8181). Bit of a hike—100 miles from D.C.—but well worth it for architecture buffs, as is the nearby University of Virginia in Charlottesville.

Mt. Vernon (Mt. Vernon, Virginia, 703-780-2000). Located 15 miles south of Washington, definitely worth a visit. No wonder Washington preferred this place to Washington. Even today, the landscape looks much like it did in his time. You can bike here via the Mount Vernon Bike Trail along the Potomac, or take a boat (554-8000 for info).

Union Station (Massachusetts and Delaware Aves, SE, 371-9441). If you didn't arrive by train, you must visit this beautifully-restored 1908 railroad temple. With its gilt and marble, it's the best-looking train station on the planet. A good place to eat and shop, too.

Dumbarton Oaks (1703 32nd St, NW, 338-8278). A famous Georgetown mansion, and the first home of the United Nations. Now houses an impressive art collection, but the exquisite gardens are the real draw. Come in spring; enter through the R St gates opposite 31st St.

Georgetown. Walk up and down the brick sidewalks, peering into the parlor windows. Stop by **Dumbarton House** (2715 Q St, 337-2288), an early Federal (c. 1799) manse open to the public, not to be confused with Dumbarton Oaks.

Main Reading Room of the Library of Congress (First St SE, 707-6400). It only takes a few minutes to view this spectacular space, a soaring octagon. Or arrange for a tour of the entire building by calling 707-5458.

Chesapeake & Ohio Canal (runs from Georgetown to Maryland). Hike or bike the towpath of this well-preserved relic. The National Park Service offers guided walks, and you can rent canoes and rowboats.

NEAR WASHINGTON: REHOBOTH BEACH, DE (AREA CODE 302)

Rehoboth Beach, Delaware is a popular getaway for residents of Philadelphia and D.C., both of which lie a two-hour drive away. Year-round population sinks from a summer high of 60,000 down to about 1,200 in winter in Rehoboth proper. About 6 or 7 guest houses, not all of them open in the off-season, cater to gay visitors. Here are the basics: the gay beach is just south of Queen St at Poodle Point (I'm not making this up). Open year-round, **Renegade** (4274 Highway One, 227-4713) is the only dance bar in town, an all-in-one complex that features a swimming pool, cabaret, and accommodations. (All the bars here have restaurants, since local liquor laws require it.) Among other guest houses: the predominantly-gay, 15-room **Sand in My Shoes** (corner of Canal and 6th, 226-2006; rates: $146-$183 for a 2-day weekend off season; $100-$146 per weekend night in season, less during the week) and the eight-room **Beach House** (15 Hickman St, 227-7074 /800-283-4667; rates: $50 off season, $90-$130 in), judged by some as the most upscale guest house, gay-friendly and -operated, but not gay-owned. Also try the 14-room (all with private bath) **Shore Inn** (703 Rehoboth Ave, 800-597-8899, rates: $35-$50 off, $75-$120 in season) and **Guest Rooms at Rehoboth** (45 Baltimore Ave, 227-8355, rates: $95-$175 summer weekends, $25 less during the week; $55-$75 off season). Choose from 10-12 gay-oriented restaurants, including gay-owned **Manos** (227-6707, entrees $10-$14) and predominantly gay (70% in summer) **Cloud Nine** (234 Rehoboth Ave, 226-1999, entrees: $7-$17, dinner only) with its eclectic bistro fare. Also very popular: **Blue Moon** (35 Baltimore Ave, 227-6515), a restaurant/bar with a crowd-pleasing happy hour. To do: Shopping along Wilmington and Baltimore Aves (plus outlet malls with no sales tax), beach, windsurfing. Other options: take the Cape May-Lewis Ferry for antiquing in Lewis, Delaware's first town (lots of historical architecture) or hike in Cape Henlopen State Park (20 minutes away). **Lambda Rising** (39 Baltimore Ave, 227-6969), the local branch of the Washington bookstore, is open year round. **Letters from Camp Rehoboth** (227-5620) is the local gay publication.

KEEP FIT/RECREATION

Strangely, Washington doesn't have a gay-owned, mostly-gay gym.

Bally's Holiday Spa (2000 L St, NW, 331-7898). Gay-popular but doesn't accept day visitors.

The Washington Sports Club (1835 Connecticut Ave NW, 332-0100). High marks for location, a short walk from Dupont Circle, and good equipment. Day fee: $20.

National Capitol YMCA (1711 Rhode Island Ave, NW, 862-9622). Accepts daily visitors only if you're a member of an out-of-town Y; popular with gay men.

EAT

Generally, any restaurant near the gay epicenter will be, by default, gay-oriented. Most are simply what-do-you-expect-for-$5.95 kind of places—useful for a quick bite.

TRES GAY

Annie's Paramount Steakhouse (1609 17th St, NW, 232-0395). Not gay-owned but many gay men and lesbians eat here. Cheap Martinis and Manhattans, seafood, pasta, prime rib, and onion rings. Bull in the

Pan, a marinated sizzling steak ($8.95) is the most popular dish. Entrees: $8-$30.

Pepper's (1527 17th St, NW, 328-8193). Informal indoor/outdoor cafe with lots of gays, including same sex couples holding hands. Although the food is just so-so and the service indifferent, this is one of those "how can you complain it's so cheap" restaurants. Avoid the lackluster Caesar salad with shrimp and the bone-dry turkey burger; stick to the pastas, like vegetarian lasagna. Entrees: under $7.

Pop Stop (1513 17th St NW, 238-0880). Coffee, tea, sandwiches, and desserts; lively gay clientele. The top floor is non-smoking and quieter than downstairs. Patrons study (as in college and graduate school) here. How appropriate, since the decor is 60's college dorm. Noisy and cruisy ground floor.

Trumpets (17th and Q Sts, NW, 232-4141). The most upmarket gay eatery, with comtemporary American cuisine. Under the same roof, there's a stylish bar of the same name. Entrees: $9-$19.

GAY FRIENDLY

Straits of Malaya (1838 18th St, NW, 483-1483). Should be called Gays of Malaya. Gay-owned, food is okay—the Laksa (noodle soup) was authentic, but that was about it. Cute waiters, 30%-40% gay clientele on our visit. Entrees: $10-$15.

Two Quail (320 Massachusetts Ave, NE, 543-8030). Located near the Capitol Hill Guest house, this is a romantic, gay-owned place with an eclectic menu (apricot stuffed pork chops with hunters sauce, bluefish Cubana with sun dried tomatoes). Midday it's popular with Congresswomen and female lobbyists who lunch; at dinner, it's sometimes all-gay, sometimes mixed. Entrees: $10-18.

TOP TABLES

Here are some of the restaurants the foodies have anointed. All are expensive, not very gay; and night owls take note, this is not New York: all stop serving around 10 or 10:30 pm, even on weekends. **Jean-Louis** (2650 Virginia Ave, NW, in the Watergate Hotel, 298-4488, fixed menu $85) is the restaurant that put Washington on the food map, with Michelin two-star Jean-Louis Palladin at the wheel; **Galileo** (1110 21st St, NW, 293-7191, entrees: $17-33), for Northern Italian fare in postmodern surroundings, within walking distance of the gay district; **Red Sage** (605 14th St, NW, 638-4444, entrees: $14-$28), multi-million dollar stage set for innovative Southwestern flavors.

PLAY/MEET

Washington offers nearly 30 clubs and bars for all tastes.

MOSTLY FOR DANCING

Badlands (1415 22nd St at P, NW, 296-0505). Popular on Fri nights (when Tracks is straight). Neon, fog, lights, even a bubble-maker. There are several bars: one on the dance floor, one with videos. Young, cute, shirts-off kind of crowd.

Tracks (1111 1st St, SE, 488-3320). Ranks as one of the best dance clubs in the gay world. Large outside deck, two dance floors, one large and one more intimate—great sound and lights. Don't come on Fri nights (straight). Sat is the busiest night of the week and officially gay, but putatively straight boys come with their girlfriends to see how the other half lives. Take a cab here—not the subway, and don't park your car; this is not a particularly safe neighborhood. Cover charge.

95

MOSTLY FOR CRUISING/DRINKING

The Circle (1629 Connecticut Ave, NW, 462-5575). One of DC's newest attractions. On three levels, bar on each floor. Disco in basement, restaurant on ground floor, second floor is cruise/disco bar. Spacious balcony overlooking Dupont Circle.

Fireplace (2161 P St, NW, 293-1293). Serious drinking bar, with big, potent, and inexpensive libations. (In fact, all DC bars offer affordable drink specials, the better to get plastered on.) Lots of TV screens here, both upstairs and down. One of DC's most popular bars, but not a good place to make new friends.

Fraternity House (2123 Twining Ct, behind 2122 P St, NW, 223-4917). A multi-personality kind of place, and DC's second-oldest gay hangout. Downstairs, it's a disco with two bars, attracting a mixed black/white younger crowd. Upstairs, you'll find two more bars, one called Arcade which some say is the friendliest bar in DC—a kind of gay "Cheers." The other is a video bar, where the barkeep has been doing the same job since 1978. There's also a porn video room which can get quite touchy-feely.

The Green Lantern (1335 Green Ct, NW, 638-5133). A.k.a. Green Latrine. Two dark and cruisy levels here, with a large bar upstairs featuring inner-city decor (chain link, black walls). Insiders say they're trying to make this the sluttiest bar in D.C. Light snacks are available.

Mr. P' s (2147 P St at 22nd, NW, 293-1064). Long-time Dupont Circle favorite; still pulls a cruisy crowd. Outdoor space hops during those hot Washington summer nights. Pinball machines, porn videos.

AFRICAN-AMERICAN

Delta Elite (3734 10th St, NE, 529-0626). After-hours spot that operates from midnight to 5 am, with great music and hot men. Weekends only.

LATINO

El Faro (2411 18th St, NW, 387-6554). For Latin men and women. Things don't start happening until the wee hours.

Lone Star West (2122 P St, NW, 822-8909). Formerly a piano bar called Friends, now a Latino bar/Mexican restaurant.

LESBIAN

Hung Jury (1819 H St, NW, 279-3212). Dance floor, video games, pool table; men are allowed if accompanied by women.

LEATHER

DC Eagle (639 New York Ave, NW, 347-605). DC's premier leather bar, although it's not that rough (many patrons don't wear the cowhide).

SEX CLUB

Club J/OE (1718 1/2 Florida Ave, NW, 328-9803). Complete with orgy room.

SHOP

Georgetown Park (3222 M St, NW, 342-8180). An impressive indoor mall with the likes of J. Crew and Ralph Lauren.

Offgear (1601 17th St, NW, 319-1157). Gay-owned clothing store with younger, fashion-forward styles.

Outlook (1706 Connecticut Ave, 745-1469). Pride items, jewelry, cards, etc.

Rock Creek (2029 P St, NW, 332-0100). Features high-style casual wear, workout, running, and swimsuits. Men wear Rock Creek logo

T-shirts as a gay badge.

Skynear & Co (2122 18th St, NW, 797-7160). This Adams-Morgan purveyor of collectibles, art, and eclectic furniture caters to a largely gay male clientele although not gay-owned. Gargoyle reproductions in plaster make a nice momento beginning at $12.50. Great sofas.

RESOURCES

This is a resource-rich community: the main gay newspaper lists two full pages of community organizations in Washington and suburbs, including nearly 60 AIDS service groups. Still, as of this writing, there is no gay tourist or chamber of commerce organization.

GENERAL INFORMATION

The Washington D.C. Convention and Visitors Association (1455 Pennsylvania Ave, NW, 789-7000). Maintains a Tourist Information Center.

Newcomer's Handbook™ for Washington, D.C. (First Books, 312-276-5911). Tremendously useful book for anyone (gay or straight) *moving* here.

GAY/HIV INFORMATION

The Whitman-Walker Clinic (797-3500). Largest AIDS organization. There is no gay and lesbian center.

BOOKSTORE

Lambda Rising (1625 Connecticut Ave, NW, 462-6969). One of the country's best gay bookstores, not only because of what they carry, but because the owners and staff make shoppers feel welcome. Books, T-shirts, posters, music, videos, and greeting cards.

PUBLICATIONS

Washington Blade (1408 U St, NW, 20009, 797-7000). Covers the Washington and national scene admirably.

Metro Arts and Entertainment Weekly (724 Ninth St, NW, 20001, 347-7640) is much smaller—entertainment and news.

Gay USA

THE RESORTS

99

FIRE ISLAND, NY

AREA CODE 516

WHAT TO EXPECT

F ire Island (strictly speaking, the communities of Fire Island Pines and Cherry Grove) is different from the other gay resorts described in this book because it's not really designed for tourists. The 32-mile-long island's relative isolation makes it hard to reach, and the fact that most summer residents rent houses rather than hotel rooms makes it expensive and inconvenient for weekenders, let alone day trippers (although you *can* come here just for the day). In fact, Cherry Grove offers only a handful of hotels and guest houses, and the Pines just two. But while this is a less than welcoming destination, with a dearth of good restaurants (everybody eats at home), it's a truly beautiful and fashionable outpost nonetheless, and worth at least one visit.

With its quaint wooden boardwalks, little red wagons (for carting groceries), and roaming, inquisitive deer, Fire Island remains fairly undeveloped. You can't bring your car here, and you won't find much to do, other than laze on the sand and stare at the gorgeous, uncrowded beaches and the even more gorgeous swarms of men, many of them self-absorbed and attitude-drenched. But for some visitors, that's enough.

Fire Island Pines and Cherry Grove are just two of 17 communities on the island, and most of Fire Island is a National Seashore, part of which offers camping facilities. So, just as in Provincetown, you can come here and not do the gay scene at all. A half-mile from Cherry Grove there's a nature walk called the Sunken Forest which is well worth a visit.

Much more than the 20 minute walk through the infamous "meat rack"—an enchanted forest of holly trees and scrub pine where men roam late at night looking for sex—separates the two gay enclaves. For A-listers, Cherry Grove is less fashionable than the Pines because it attracts more women, tacky drag queens, gawking straight daytrippers, and unfashionable Long Island gays—people who have been living in their parents' basement for the last 45 years. The houses in the Grove are closer together, quainter, and smaller. Manhattanites go to the Pines, where life revolves around exclusive, see-and-be-seen house parties in expensive, modern beach-front homes, some of which are in imminent danger of falling into the ocean thanks to beach erosion.

Probably the best way to experience Fire Island is to rent a house and have your own see-and-be-seen party. To make it economical, get a group of friends together, or surf the internet (e.g., America Online under Gay and Lesbian/Travel headings) to find a "share"—a part-time rental with a group of other people.

BEST TIME TO COME

The busiest times are major holiday weekends, such as the 4th of July when the "Invasion of the Pines" happens, and the weekend of the Gay Men's Health Crisis (GHMC) Morning Party each August. Rates are much lower mid-week, before Memorial Day, and after Labor Day.

GETTING AROUND

Everyone walks here since private cars are banned. There's a water taxi (589-0822, approx. $10) between the Pines and the Grove.

GETTING THERE

Getting here is half the battle. During summer, the **Sayville Ferry Service** (589-0810) run frequently between Sayville, Long Island and both Fire Island Pines and Cherry Grove ($10 roundtrip, 20 minutes). Sayville lies 80 minutes from New York City via the Long Island Railroad. Vans or taxis meet the trains to bring people to the ferry. A company called Islanders Club (212-663-8898) runs buses from Thu to Mon to/from Manhattan. You can also fly into Islip's MacArthur Airport and take a 20 min. cab ride (rates vary, Colonial Taxi is cheapest) to the ferry dock.

STAY

FIRE ISLAND PINES

Botel (The Pines, 597-6500). One of the few accommodations for transients in the Pines, and they treat you that way. Twenty-five rooms, truly unappealing cinder block atmosphere. Rates: $275 weekends; weekday rates $55 with shared bath, $65 with private.

Pines Place (The Pines, 597-6162). The best place to stay in the Pines—not really a guest house, more like a nightly or weekly share. Quarry tile floors and rough pine walls throughout. Hot tub but no pool. Seven guest rooms. Rates: in season, $95 weekdays $200 weekends (higher on holiday weekends, lower before Memorial Day and after Labor Day).

CHERRY GROVE

Most of the island's transient accommodations are in Cherry Grove.

The Belvedere (PO Box 4026, Cherry Grove, 597-6448). An old mansion with character topped with towers and domes from various architectural periods, probably the best option in either the Pines or Cherry Grove. Forty rooms away from the crowds. Gay men only. Open until mid-October. Rates: during week $80-$100 double, weekends (two night min.) $300-$400.

Carousel Guest House (185 Holly Walk, 597-6612). Adjoining a disco. Tres basic for those who like to be near the action. Rates: Call.

The Cherry Grove Beach Club (Bayview Walk, Cherry Grove, 597-6600). Fifty-seven rooms, 16 of which are classified deluxe. Not directly on beach. Ice Palace disco is attached. Closes for season late Sept. Rates: $80-$120 during week; weekends 2 night min. $300-$400.

103

Dune Point (Lewis Walk, 597-6261). Only place open year round. Rooms and apartments with private and shared baths. Plusses here are the right-on-the-beach location and friendly management, but thin sheets and uncomfortable mattresses—could use spiffing up. Rates: start at $55 off season, $75 in, $395 for three nights (minimum) on holiday weekends.

REAL ESTATE AGENTS

Rental rates begin at around $1,500 a week and go up—and up—from there. If there are enough of you, it can work.

Bob Howard (597-9400).

Hanlan's (597-9630).

Island Properties (597-6360).

Pines Harbor (597-7575).

SEE/DO

Fire Island supports a wide range of wildlife, and a brief walk will expose you to it. You'll encounter deer, marshes, and a National Seashore with scrub pine and a boardwalk leading to a ranger's station and visitor's area.

THE ROUTINE

The weekend routine begins on Fri evening with drinks and dancing at the Island Club in the Pines, followed by high tea upstairs at the Pavilion which begins around 8 pm. This is the time for socializing and trying to break through the attitude to meet people. Have dinner between 9:30 and 11 pm. Then get your hand stamped at the Pavilion, but don't go in until after midnight. Dance until dawn, straggle home. Around noon, get up and straggle to the beach. Later in the pm, go to the gym, primp, and repeat Fri night's ritual.

KEEP FIT/RECREATION

Island Gym (between the Boatel and the Pavillion, The Pines. No phone). Gym in a tent. Day fee: $10.

EAT

Michael's (Bayview Walk, Cherry Grove, 597-6555). Although the decor is luncheonette, this is considered one of the better restaurants. Breakfast, lunch, dinner; waiters without attitude. Mostly gay clientele. Entrees: $10-$19.

Top of the Bay (Bayview Walk, Cherry Grove). Probably the best restaurant in Cherry Grove and The Pines. Fabulous sunset views, international cuisine with emphasis on seafood. Dinner and Sun brunch. Entrees: $18-$26.

The Yacht Club at the Boatel (The Pines, 597-6131). Tries for a formal atmosphere with large, wide-spaced tables. Although I didn't eat here, no one I talked to said anything good about the food. A bar called the **Blue Whale** is also found here. Order the special. Entrees: $10-18.

PLAY/MEET

MOSTLY FOR DANCING

The Pavilion (The Dock, Fire Island Blvd, The Pines 597-6677). Late night crowd goes until the wee hours. The premier dance spot with men-to-die-for.

Ice Palace (Beach Hotel, Cherry Grove, 597-6600). Mostly men. Not nearly as A-list as the Pavilion, attracting a lot of curious straights these days.

MOSTLY FOR CRUISING/DRINKING

Island Club (The Pines). Shiny white wood floors, lots of windows and light. Small dance floor, piano, pool table, great deck upstairs. Popular on Fri nights.

SHOP

Overtures (Fire Island Blvd, The Pines, 597-4201). Nice selection of gifts, tableware, candles, cards.

All American Boy (in the Pavillion/Island Club complex, The Pines, 597-7758). Outpost of the popular men's clothing store.

RESOURCES

105

GENERAL INFORMATION

In keeping with its untouristy nature, there is no visitor info bureau, gay chamber of commerce, or anything of the kind.

KEY WEST, FLORIDA

AREA CODE 305

WHAT TO EXPECT

People who are visiting Key West for the first time invariably have the same reaction: it's not quite what they thought. Comparisons with Provincetown are inevitable and may help you understand what Key West is and isn't. Both resorts lie at the end of a long drive. Both have a large gay population. But Key West is more of a real city than Provincetown will ever be, with all of the good and bad that implies. Key West has traffic lights, a crime problem, bars on windows, a crack trade, crime-watch neighborhoods, homeless people, public transportation, and parking meters. It has a real airport with American Eagle and USAir Express flights. It's also more upscale: not just the guest houses, which are in general more sophisticated than what Provincetown has to offer, but the shopping is more upmarket, too, with brand names like Timberland and the Gap. And while Provincetown certainly has its share of straights, gays seem to predominate there. "Gays made Key West and gays will break it," one long-time local, a straight, told me. But very rarely did I see two gays or lesbians holding hands while walking down the street here; in Provincetown, with its unique spirit and energy, such public display of affection is a common sight. Strolling down Duval Street at night, your ears are assaulted by music blaring out from the straight clubs, as one band tries to out-amplify the other. Amid this migraine-inducing chaos, a rowdy younger crowd competes for sidewalk with older straight couples.

Of course, the big thing that Key West has over Provincetown is warm winter weather. In fact, this subtropical island's climate is enjoyable 365 days a year. Although it does get humid, the highest temperature ever recorded was a livable 97 degrees, with an all-time low of 40. The temperate climate has helped make the Conch Republic an increasingly year-round destination.

Key West wasn't always this way. In the 70's, the town was just locals and gays, with a few straight college students thrown in. Now the place is more mainstream—cruise ships, fast food, Middle America. As a result perhaps most gay visitors retreat behind the walls of the town's luxurious guest houses which, as we shall see, is a pretty enviable fate, hanging around the many azure pools. In addition, South Beach has drawn away potential visitors. Some say that Key West is just as gay as ever: there are more gay guest houses than before, and just as many gay tourists. Perhaps that's true, but there are even more straight tourists, and the gay percentage has been diluted. Whatever. It's worth a trip, and you'll find plenty to do—or not do.

BEST TIME TO COME

Winter.

GETTING THERE

The 3-4 hour drive from Miami to Key West is a pleasant experience, unless you're stuck behind a lumbering Winnebago. You might want to drive one way and fly out the other—American Eagle and USAir Express are two options. (It helps that there are no drop off charges for one-way rentals in Florida). A cab from the airport to town costs $5-6. Call 296-6666.

GETTING AROUND

You don't need wheels here. Drop off your rental car (Budget will drive you back to town from their airport and Highway 1 locations) and instead, rent bikes or scooters from **Moped Hospital** (601 Truman Ave, 296-3344).

STAY

The Conch Republic sets the standard of quality for gay guest houses. No other major gay destination can boast this many luxurious, comfortable, and attractive options. You can choose from over 40 gay-oriented properties, most with romantic rooms, friendly staff, and a festive atmosphere. Not surprisingly, rates are much higher in winter than in summer. Several places stand out:

MOSTLY GAY

Alexander's (1118 Fleming St, 294-9919 or 800-654-9919). The kind of place where when you walk in everyone sitting around the pool will look up and smile and say hello. Behind its buzz-in wooden fence, an oasis of calm in a central location. Fifteen rooms scattered in several two-story clapboard buildings nestled around a relaxing pool. French doors open from rooms onto a deck or terrace; above each door a custom-made stained glass transom depicts an island theme. Friendly staff; mixed crowd: mostly gay and lesbian, but some straights now and then, with wide age range. Low sexual energy: good place for couples, but many singles here too. Rates: $80 (summer season, 1/2 bath)-$165 (high season, deluxe cottage).

Big Ruby's (409 Applerouth La, 296-2323 or 1-800-477-RUBY). This collection of attractive clapboard two- and three-story buildings ranks as one of the three or four best guest houses in town. Excellent breakfast, charming owners. Flagstone and wood deck surrounds a palm-fringed pool; one night my friend Allen and I returned to discover the pool gurgling, the white miniature lights twinkling, a breeze rustling through the palms, and Enya's *Caribbean Blue* floating over the sound system— pretty darn romantic. Try to get room 5, overlooking the pool and lush greenery from a third floor aerie. Rates: $68-$103 summer, $110-$160 winters and holidays.

The Brass Key (412 Frances Street, 296-4719). If Ritz-Carlton opened a gay guest house, this is what it would be like. The professionalism of the staff (the owner was a hotel executive in a previous life), the handsome decor, and big-hotel touches like dataport phones, remote color TV, thick terry towels, and turn down service are what set the Brass Key apart. Seems to attract an exceptionally friendly roster of guests who come back year after year to laze around the medium-sized pool and whirlpool, both of which are conducive to intimate and romantic conversation. Rates (vary by size of bed and season): Kings $105-$150; queens $95-$140; double $85-$130.

La Te Da (1125 Duval, 296-6706). Once the hottest property in Key West, had declined over the years along with its owners' fortunes. It's now in much better shape: popular bar, restaurant, tea dance venue, and inn. Rooms here look inviting: gleaming hard wood floors, Floridaish rattan furnishings, and attractive fabrics. A decent restaurant surrounds the pool terrace. The restaurant, bar (popular Fri happy hour with excellent pina coladas) and disco attract a mostly-gay crowd, making this a must-visit place. Rates: $60-$80 off season, $100-$125 in season, higher during holidays and special events.

FOR MEN ONLY

Curry House (806 Fleming St, 294-6777 or 800-633-7439). One of the few exclusively male upscale havens, which distinguishes it from some of the other luxe properties. Most of the 19 rooms have private baths, all with decks or verandah space but aren't of the same standard as Alexander's, the Brass Key, and Big Ruby's. Oldest guest house on the island, one of the most popular—booking a year or two in advance for high season dates is advised. Less sexual tension and more camaraderie than at other all-male houses—the kind of place where 15 guests, strangers a couple of days ago, will organize dinner together. No phones or TVs (owners claims guests don't want them). Rates: $115-$145 in high season, $80-$100 in low season.

Island House for Men (1129 Fleming St, 294-6284 or 800-890-6284). Famed for high sexual atmosphere rather than the quality of the 34 guest rooms (12 with private bath). X-rated video room with strategically-placed rolls of paper towels—capisce? Large, wood-decked pool around which breakfast and lunch served. Rates: $65-$110 off season, $85-$145 in season (depending on room size and whether private bath or not).

Lighthouse Court (902 Whitehead, 294-9588). You've seen the ads for years—the cute young stud with the smooth chest and towel around his neck. At 42 rooms, the largest all-male clothing-optional resort. Rooms have been brightened up recently, but the place still suffers from thin towel syndrome. High sexual energy a la Palm Springs creates a certain tension among guests. The Jacuzzi gets very—how you say—*festive* late at night. Only one of two places serving lunch poolside (Island House for Men is the other); tasty food, reasonable prices. On our visit, guests were having fun—perhaps a little too much fun for those who weren't part of the frolic. Not in the best neighborhood (barbed wire along the fence): be careful coming and going at night. Rates: $90-$150 off season, $125-$235 in season.

Newton Street Station (1414 Newton St, 294-4288 or 800-248-2457). Seven rooms including one efficiency, 4 with private bath. Notable for its friskiness. Popular with leathermen. Rates: $75-$110.

Oasis Guest House (823 Fleming, 296-2131). Upmarket and attractive—the best exclusively-male property. Some rooms offer VCRs; suites with wine and cheese on check-in. Favorite rooms are 8, 9, and 19 (book way ahead). Nightly turn-down service, a beer and wine honor bar, and little surprises like a free barbecue or fashion show. Community spirit prevails, with an attractive swimming pool plus a separate volleyball pool. Work by a local artist adorns the walls on rotating basis. Rates: $75-$120 off season, $100-$170 in season.

GAY-FRIENDLY

Simonton Court (320 Simonton St, 294-6386). Knockout accommodations, but don't come here if looking for high gay content. Originally built in 1880 as a Cuban cigar factory. Some rooms in original workers' cabins, now lovingly restored as two-bedroom cottages; others in the Mansion House, former home of plantation owner. Latter are gorgeous and have everything: gleaming wood floors, wine and cheese on check-in, a Bose sound system with 30-channel cable radio, a Jacuzzi in the bedroom, private widow's walk with to-die-for sunsets—in other words, all the ingredients for a romantic stay. Rates: $100-$170 for regular rooms, $180-$200 for cottages sleeping 4-6; $150-$250/$280-$350 in season.

SEE/DO

TEN THINGS NO SELF-RESPECTING GAY PERSON SHOULD MISS

There's more of a cultural nature to do and see on this four-by-two-mile island than in most gay resorts, so leave yourself time.

"Miss Sunshine" sunset cruises (on the shoreline between Waterfront Market and the Turtle Kraals Tower, 296-4608). The most fun you'll have in Key West. Everyone's in a great mood on this gay party boat, fueled by the free beer and wine. After the sun goes down, the stripper does things they don't do on land.

Conch Tour Train (501 Front Street, 294-5161). Kitschy but useful.

Mallory Square. An old Key West tradition during which sidewalk entertainers and tourists gather to watch the sunset. A sign in front of Billie's Bar indicates when the sun will set.

The Ernest Hemingway House (907 Whitehead St, 294-1515). Built in 1851, is a registered historic landmark, the long-time residence of Papa H. It now houses the writer's mementos from around the world.

The Little White House Museum (111 Front St, 294-9911). Where Harry Truman spent 175 days of his 6 1/2 year presidency.

The Mel Fisher Maritime Museum (200 Greene St, 294-2633). Shipwreck artifacts.

The Audubon House and Tropical Gardens (205 Whitehead St, 294-1575). Audubon never lived or even slept in this 19th century home, but he did visit, and his prints, collected by Capt. John Geiger, are everywhere.

Red Barn Theater (319 Duval St, 296-9911). For something cultural, the 60-seat stages quality productions of musicals and dramas, including some written by locals.

The Tennessee Williams Fine Arts Center (5901 Junior College Rd, 296-9081). Another cultural venue, and the Bauhaus-style theater is itself worth touring.

Take a walk. Notice the conch (pronounced "conk") houses, the original ones built without nails. Strict preservation laws govern exterior renovation: you can't repaint your house the same color without permission, and a separate tree commission controls the planting, removal, and pruning of arboreal specimens.

THE ROUTINE

Key West lacks the rigid routine of a Provincetown, where tea dance is a daily affair in summer (here, tea happens only on Sun). The ritual begins at La-Te-Da's (see under **Stay**) for early tea (5 to 8 pm), then the crowd moves to the Atlantic Shores (8-11 pm), and then migrates to the Copa for dancing from 11 pm until whenever. On other days, it's wake up at 9-10, breakfast in your guest house, then off to the beach or lazing around the pool until nap time. Later one might have drinks at LaTeDa's, followed by dinner around 9, and dancing at the Copa.

KEEP FIT/RECREATION

112

Higgs Beach offers $5 chair rentals; its "Dick Dock" is known for semi-nude sunbathing.

Ft. Taylor Beach is rockier but still attractive; bike or scooter there.

Duval Square Health & Fitness (1075 Duval St at Virginia, 292-9683). Best gay-oriented gym. Day fee: $12.

Lighthouse Court (see above). Small but everything you need. Cruisy. Day fee: $10.

SPECIAL EVENTS

Fantasy Fest (296-1817). Longest-running event in town: ten days in late October with street fairs, lots of drag, and a parade.

Key West Gay Arts Festival (800-429-9759). Lectures, exhibitions, performances, and other events. Happens each June.

EAT

Restaurants here are abundant and many are excellent, but tend to be pricey. None have a predominantly gay clientele; all are mixed.

GAY-FRIENDLY

Antonia's (615 Duval St, 294-6565). Upscale Italian, one of the best on the island, with a mostly-straight clientele. Main dishes like homemade linguine tossed with shrimp, scallops, mussels, fresh tomato, and olive oil are all winners. Entrees: $12-$22.

Café Marquesa (600 Fleming St in the Marquesa Hotel, 292-1244). Most visitors I polled said this was their favorite restaurant. Small, pricey but enticing menu, with entrees like grilled shrimp with roasted banana-red curry sauce escorted by crisp sweet potato fritters and fresh mango relish, and sesame-encrusted rack of lamb with coconut-mint pesto and wild mushroom cous-cous. Entrees: $17-$26.

La Terraza (1125 Duval St, 294-2943). Part of the La-Te-Da hotel/bar complex, tasty new-American cuisine, large portions, friendly waiters. Entrees: $12-$17.

La Trattoria Venezia (524 Duval St, 296-1075). Not the place to go for a quiet tete-a-tete; nothing but hard surfaces here. Gay-owned, but clientele on our visit consisted mostly of boisterous straights. Tasty Northern Italian cuisine, with emphasis on seafood. Entrees: $12-$25.

Louie's Back Yard (700 Waddell Ave, 294-1061). Locals say it's overpriced, and the wonderful waterfront setting is best enjoyed at lunch, when prices are lower, or for drinks. Entrees: $24-$30.

Square One (1075 Duval St in the Duval Square complex, 296-4300). Elegant and expensive. Features new American cuisine, including fresh seafood. Clientele is mixed gay-straight, but you can be fairly comfortable holding hands. A pianist adds extra atmosphere. Entrees: $18-20.

CHEAP EATS

Camille's (703 1/2 Duval at Anaela St, 296-4811). Gay-owned, serves breakfast all day (wonderful home-baked muffins, get here by 9 am to avoid a line), and is useful for an inexpensive dinner (Tue through Sat nights only). Entrees: $9-$15.

The Twisted Noodle (628 Duval St, 296-6670). Even though locals recommend it highly, it won't have you dashing off postcards to the folks back home. Features satisfying but forgettable Italian food at decent prices in an outdoor setting. A typical main course (and many of them sound the same) might be chicken, artichoke hearts, and broccoli served in a cream tomato sauce over linguine. Entrees: $7.50-$15.

PLAY/MEET

Clubs and bars start late (around 11 pm) and go until the wee hours. There isn't the huge variety you'd find in a large city, but there's enough. The good news: patrons are much friendlier here than in South Beach.

MOSTLY FOR DANCING

Atlantic Shores (305 South St, 296-2491). Popular "Tea by the Sea" tea dances on Sun. Also a recently-redecorated motel, but you probably won't want to stay here unless you like to be in the center of the hubbub.

Club Chameleon/Flamingo Follies (524 Eaton St, 296-3030). Church-turned-disco and cabaret. The mostly-straight audience seemed to enjoy the Follies, an embarrassingly clunky locally-themed revue, but if you're like me you'll need several drinks or something stronger to endure it. After, there's disco dancing until 4 am, which may give the Copa (below) a run for its money.

The Copa (623 Duval, 296-8521). Destroyed by fire in August 1995 but scheduled to reopen in spring of 1996. Will probably still import to-die-for male strippers from Miami and regain its status as the main dance venue.

114

MOSTLY FOR DRINKING/CRUISING

Club I (900 Simonton St, 296-9230). As in Club International. Small dance floor, video, small stage with occasional entertainment. Large lesbian contingent.

801 Duval (801 Duval, 294-4737). Heavy local scene, friendly, on two floors. Drab decor. Open from 11 am to 4 am. Pre-Tea Bingo on Sun.

Numbers (Truman & Francis Sts, 296-0333). Caters to older crowd who drool over the cute and cooperative strippers.

One Saloon (524 Duval, 296-8118). Three bars, small dance floor, outdoor patio. Male strip shows keep the boys happy, as do weekly drink specials.

SHOP

Shopping here is quite sophisticated, although there are a number of T-shirt and electronics emporia.

The Annex (705 Duval, 296-9800). Gay-owned, features fashionable menswear and swimwear.

Fast Buck Freddie's (500 Duval St, 294-2007). Local institution for cards, fridge magnets, frames, and gifts.

Leather Master (418a Applerouth Lane, 292-5051). Bills itself as a toy shop for the adventurous. Come here for leatherware, books and magazines, and all the usual paraphernalia.

Sandcastles (1219 Duval St, 292-3048). Gay-pride items, affordable gifts.

Virgin Key West (429 Caroline at Duval, 294-0555). Housed in an historic house and offers locally-made, whimsically-patterned shirts and shorts, including a fetching flying pigs design. Sponsors fashion shows in local guest houses.

RESOURCES

GENERAL INFORMATION

Key West Business Guild (424 Fleming St, 800-535-7797 or 294-4603). Gay chamber of commerce. Good source for free info.

The Key West Welcome Center (3840 N. Roosevelt Blvd, 296-4444). Provides general tourist information, including self-guided walking tour maps.

GAY/HIV INFORMATION

AIDS Help (296-6196). Private non-profit organization offering anonymous testing and free condoms.

AIDS Prevention Center (513 Whitehead, 292-6701).

BOOKSTORE

Caroline Street Books (800 Caroline St, 294-3931). Now that A Bookstore Named Desire is closed, this gay-owned store is it. Offers more than just gay-themed books. Coffee bar.

PUBLICATIONS

There is no serious gay press here.

Southern Exposure Guide (819 Peacock Plaza, 294-6303). A useful monthly for entertainment schedules.

Gay Press/the Pride Connection (292-0061) is a small weekly publication.

Channel 5, the local outlet for TCI Cablevision, carries some gay programming.

NEW HOPE, PA

AREA CODE 215

WHAT TO EXPECT

People might tell you that New Hope is a sleepy little town consisting of two streets and that there's not much to do here except poke your nose in the stores. Actually, there's a lot more to this peaceful, bucolic hideaway on the Delaware River. Located just 90 minutes from New York and 45 from Philadelphia, New Hope is an easy day trip from either metropolis. This proximity explains why many gay men are "dropping out" of the urban rat race and setting up shop (or B&B) here.

But they haven't brought all the woes of the big city with them. People don't bolt their houses shut in New Hope (one innkeeper laughed when I locked the doors to my rental car—"honey, get with the program, this isn't Philly!"). The year-round population hovers around 1,200, with perhaps 25% gay.

Despite the heavy gay presence, this place doesn't enjoy anything close to the openness you'd find in Provincetown or New York's Fire Island. Gay life here is much more closeted—no hand holding down the main street. On my visit, one gay B&B owner wouldn't discuss his operation in front of a straight workman. "People blend in here; there are no activists or Act Uppers," this innkeeper told me. "New Hope has become more tolerant and progressive over the years, but gays don't flaunt it here."

New Hope is a physically attractive place. Local planners have banned anything garish or tacky. It's all very tasteful, perhaps a little too much so. And although there's lots to do, you probably wouldn't come here for a week as you would Provincetown, unless you use New Hope as a base for exploring Amish country, Philadelphia, the surrounding countryside, and, just across the Delaware River in New Jersey, little towns with names like Lumberville, Erwinna and Frenchtown that time has forgotten. Or almost forgotten. Locals remind you that Sally Jesse Raphael's daughter died nearby, and Jessica Savitch, the ill-starred network news reporter, drowned in the Delaware Canal along with her dog and husband not far from town. Celebrities come and go and buy the cute fieldstone farm houses and renovate them and everyone tries to mind their own business.

BEST TIME TO COME

Every season has its charms.

GETTING THERE

Easy 45 minute drive from Philadelphia, or 90 minute drive from Manhattan, traffic permitting.

GETTING AROUND

In town, by foot. By car everywhere else.

STAY

GAY

The Lexington House (6171 Upper York Rd, 215-794-0811). A class act, and the only exclusively gay-clienteled and gay-owned B&B in the New Hope area. This six-room property features wide plank floors, antiques or repros in the rooms, a pool built from the fieldstone foundation of the old barn, seven acres of privacy, and an affable proprietor—Alex Febles, who has lived here for 15 years. Low sexual temperature—not great for singles; come here with your lover. Rates: $75-$160.

GAY-FRIENDLY

Backstreet Inn (144 Old York Rd, 862-9571). Gay-owned but a mixed clientele (sometimes 100% straight—you takes your chances). Seven attractive but smallish rooms with updated decor, private baths, extensive breakfast. Rates: $120.

The Raven (385 W. Bridge St, 862-2081). This bar, motel, B&B, and restaurant gets mobbed on Sun. The motel rooms are dreary, but do have private baths, unlike accommodations in the guest house. People go from room to room knocking on doors and some guests keep the blinds open advertising their wares. Not a place for couples, unless you're into a certain scene. Attractive pool area. Rates: $69-$89.

Fox & Hound (246 W. Bridge St, 862-5082). Gay-owned but doesn't cater exclusively to gay clientele (approx. half and half). Five comfortable, clean rooms with private baths in 1850's restored fieldstone house. Central location, friendly owner. Rates: around $110 weekends, $60-80 midweek.

SEE/DO

TEN THINGS NO SELF-RESPECTING GAY PERSON SHOULD MISS

Antiquing in New Hope and surrounding areas.

Bucks County Playhouse (70 S. Main St, 862-2041). Summer stock—William Shatner, Loretta Swit, etc.

New Hope & Ivyland Steam Railroad (West Bridge St and Stockton Ave, 862-2332). An antique steam train full of nostalgia.

Mule Barge on the Delaware Canal (New and S. Main Sts, 862-2842). Gay-owned attraction.

Parry Mansion (S. Main and Ferry Sts, 862-5308). Historic home built in 1784 by New Hope's leading citizen.

119

River Road through Lumberville. Pleasant drive through one of the most attractive towns in the Northeast.

Tinicum Arts Festival (610-294-9420). Every July.

James A. Michener Art Museum (138 S. Pine St, Doylestown, 340-9800).

Peddler's Village (Lahaska, PA, 794-4000). Over 70 boutiques and restaurants, too cute or charming–you decide.

Pennsbury Manor (400 Pennsbury Memorial Rd, Morrisville, PA, 946-0400). Pre-Revolutionary home of William Penn, lots of fine antiques.

KEEP FIT/RECREATION

Gym rats will have to resort to push ups and jogging.

EAT

TRES GAY

The Cartwheel (437 York Rd, 862-0880). The Rainbow Grille serves surprisingly decent fare like crabcakes with jalapeno tartar sauce, roasted duck topped with black-cherry Grand Marnier sauce and—the house specialty—rigatoni a la vodka. Entrees: $9–$18.

The Raven (385 W. Bridge St, 862-2081). This one-stop-shopping restaurant/bar/motel offers solid cooking in a clubby, oak-panelled atmosphere. Entrees: $17-$20.

The Café (Rtes 519 and 604, Rosemont, NJ, 609-397-4097). Lesbian-owned, 50% gay/lesbian clientele. Serves dinner Wed-Sun only, breakfast and lunch most other days; weekend brunch is very gay and the busiest time. Blackboard specials, lots of fish, chicken, and vegetarian entrees such as spicy peanut chicken pasta. Homemade desserts. Staff mostly gay and lesbian. Entrees: $9-17; fixed price menus hover around $13 for 2-3 courses.

GAY-FRIENDLY

Evermay-on-the-Delaware (River Road, Erwinna, PA, 610-294-9100). Located just south of the Frenchtown Bridge, this culinary adventure centers around a six-course set feast with Champagne. Entrees like roast loin of veal with lentils. Fri, Sat, Sun and some holidays. Set menu: $48 per person.

PLAY/MEET

MOSTLY FOR DANCING

The Cartwheel (see above). Rocks at night, especially on Sat, with several bars (one non-smoking) and a good-sized dance floor, plus piano bar and outside space.

MOSTLY FOR CRUISING/DRINKING

The Raven (see above) is the only choice; also features dancing.

SHOP

Grownups (2 E. Mechanic St, 862-9304). Sexy silk lingerie, latex and leather toys, x-rated videos for rent and sale, x-rated cards.

Class Act (127-B S. Main St, 862-5330). Gay-owned. Carefully-edited casual clothing for men, including 2 x ist underwear.

Mystical Tymes (127 S. Main St, 862-5629). Gay-owned New Age shop with crystals, herbs, etc.

RESOURCES

GENERAL INFORMATION

New Hope Chamber of Commerce (PO Box 633; 862-5880).

PALM SPRINGS, CA

AREA CODE 619

WHAT TO EXPECT

Although Palm Springs is blessed with fine weather, especially outside the blistering summer months, all is not paradise. The area sits squarely on the San Andreas Fault, and in June 1992 a 7.2 quake emptied pools and sent wall hangings flying. Smog darkens the skies ("We call it haze," a local booster explained) and although crime is low compared to Los Angeles, some residents do put bars on their windows, even in the ubiquitous "gated" communities. Over-watering of golf courses, the creation of green parks, gardens, and lawns, and the importation of moisture-guzzling non-native flora have lowered the water table, interfering with delicate desert ecosystems, while also creating one of the very things people visit this desert clime to escape: humidity. "We sit on the largest aquifer in North America," one local told me. "Even if we doubled our growth, it would last for 400 years." But what about after that, I wondered? Apres-nous, le drought? Later, at the Living Desert Museum (**See/Do,** below) I discover that watering all those golf courses, including the full-size one surrounding *TV Guide* mogul Walter Annenberg's estate, is indeed screwing up the environment.

Straight people come here for two things: golf and heat. Gays and lesbians come here for low-key relaxation in comfortable guest houses. In the mid-80's there were fewer than 10 gay hotels. Today, over 30 compete for guests, and more are on the way. So there's something for everyone, and each place reflects the particular taste of its owners. The key differentiators are price, size, location, and sexual friskiness. Most guest houses are located in Palm Springs' Warm Sands neighborhood, within walking distance of many bars and downtown. (Everything is fairly close to everything else, so location shouldn't be your first concern.) A few are in Cathedral City or north of downtown Palm Springs.

What we call "Palm Springs" is really an amalgamation of several distinct communities with their own governing bodies and police forces. For our purposes the important ones are Palm Springs itself, and neighboring Cathedral City, home to many gay bars and restaurants and several hotels (Cathedral City's Cove area is the gay residential district, if one can be said to exist).

Although each city has its own flavor, no matter where you go you'll find the things that attracted gay settlers in the first place: meticulously-maintained, wide, palm-lined boulevards; and a distinct lack of urban ills, including litter, graffiti, and short tempers. The homeless seem to have been magically exorcised.

Today, Palm Springs is a great place to escape winter's cold, a pleasant alternative to muggy, buggy Florida or the Caribbean, where sometimes unfriendly natives and high prices can make travel a travail. It's also worth considering if you're about to retire: real estate is inexpensive (thanks to cheap water and land, average home prices hover around $100,000), and you'll be in good company.

BEST TIME TO COME

Peak season is from mid-Mar to May; Easter weekend is packed with gorgeous men from LA and San Diego; the week of the Dinah Shore Golf Classic (late Mar) is popular with lesbians.

GETTING THERE

Palm Springs is an easy two-hour drive from LA. Or you can fly (all major airlines serve Palm Springs from their respective hubs). Upon landing, you immediately sense you're not in Boston or Boise or even LA anymore: there's an emerald putting green in the airport waiting area, complete with golf clubs and balls, so amuse yourself before taking off.

GETTING AROUND

Unlike South Beach, you'll definitely need a car here. The local **Thrifty** franchise offers two locations (328-8812 or 323-2212). There is no public transit worth mentioning. Renting a mountain bike is also an option, depending on where you're staying. Try **Canyon Bicycles** (327-7688).

STAY

GAY/BEST BEDS

Harlow Club (175 E. El Alameda, 320-4333, 800-223-4073). Low sexual energy place for those who prefer luxury to a festive, frolicky atmosphere. Large rooms, each with decks or other outdoor space, some with gas fireplaces. Other amenities: TVs/VCRs, large video library, king or queen beds with soft-as-a-cloud down comforters and pillows and crisp white sheets. Decor includes field stone floors, gray carpeting, bleached wood ceilings, white stucco walls. Free bike use, small gym, individual fridges with a bottle of Chardonnay and snacks, breakfast and lunch around the pool each day, including beer and wine. Beautiful pool and grounds. Pick up from airport if requested. Rates: $135 for the smallest room up to $260 for a suite sleeping four.

Abbey West (772 Prescott Circle, 320-4333, 800-223-4073). Single story white stucco units with black accents around an inviting pool. On our visit, the guests were younger and more attractive than at the Harlow. The room decor is deco, not California bungalow. Wall-to-wall gray carpeting in rooms, which are bigger than Harlow's. Built originally by two male comedians as their weekend getaway, the main house survives, with the bungalows added on in back. Rates: $135-$250.

Hacienda en Sueno (586 Warm Sands Dr, 327-8111, 800-359-2007). The most luxurious property in the Warm Sands area. Two pools, both beautiful, and two wings—one decorated like an 80's New York apartment (wall-to-wall, chrome and glitter), one with older furniture and tile floors, both spacious (all rooms have private patios, cooking facilities, some working fireplaces). VCRs, direct dial phones with free local calls, and exceptionally nice management are bonuses. Nude sunbathing is allowed anywhere. Rates: $165 per night in season, $59-$119 off season.

125

GAY

Shorter on luxury, but still more than comfortable:

Alexander Resort (598 Grenfall Rd, 327-6911). In the Warm Sands area, eight rooms, most with kitchenettes, beautiful grounds, inviting pool, and friendly management, which largely explains a 75% return rate and a bulletin board full of thank you notes. Fairly high sexual energy, fueled no doubt by VCRs with an x-rated gay movie channel. Rates: $79, $89, or $99 (the highest price buys a deluxe studio with kitchen and patio—well worth it).

Camp Palm Springs (722 San Lorenzo Rd, 322-CAMP or 800-793-0063). Larger (24 unit) property. Above-average furnishings, rooms on two levels arranged around a good-sized pool with a mountain backdrop. No lawns. Nice living room area. Sexual temperature: not a place to bring Aunt Millie, although most guests are couples. Friendly management. Differentiator: regulation size tennis court. Rates: most rooms are $99-$109 during the week, $20 more on weekends; three-bedroom townhouse goes for $259-$299 per night.

The Columns (537 Grenfall Rd, 325-0655, 800-798-0655). Seven smallish rooms, arranged on one level around attractively-landscaped pool. Typical client is in mid-30s, coupled, here to relax, not to perform sexual aerobics. VCRs, tape library, friendly and fun hosts. Good value for money. Rates: studios $55 Sun-Thu, $75 other days; larger rooms are $85 high season and on weekends, $70 other times.

Desert Palms Inn (67-580 East Palm Canyon Dr, Cathedral City, 324-3000). Center of activity where everyone congregates around the large pool and expansive lawn, using it like a public beach. One of two places allowing non-residents to use facilities, which include popular bar and café. Holiday Inn-ish rooms need updating; all have direct phones, color TV, and A/C. Property no longer gay owned. Rates: $40-$119.

Desert Paradise Hotel (615 Warm Sands Dr, 320-5650). Some of the best landscaping in the desert, 12 units arranged horseshoe-style on one level around pool. Modern furnishings remodeled in 1992, VCRs, most with kitchenettes, "concierge-in-a-binder" a useful touch. Rates: $95-$165.

Five-Fifty (550 Warm Sands Dr, 320-7144, 800-669-0550). The owner may answer the door wearing nothing but a leather vest, and porn films are shown in the public area—need I say more? Rates: $60.

Inntrigue (526 Warm Sands Dr, 323-7505). One of best values in Palm Springs and a top choice in the Warm Sands area. Super-friendly management attracts a fun crowd (during an evening stroll through the Warm Sands area one night I discovered that the all the laughs were originating here); with recent acquisition of property next door, now has 28 clean, high-tech rooms with new TVs and VCRs, two pools, evening happy hour, and other amenities. Rates: around $75.

Inn Exile (960 Camino Parocela, 800-962-0186). Stylish and sexually frisky place with friendly management, complimentary breakfast, lunch, and happy hour, direct dial phones, VCRs, king-sized beds, a useful fitness room, and up-to-date decor. Their slick, elaborate brochure will give you a good idea of what to expect. Rates: begin at around $80 a night.

Mirage (555 Grenfall Rd, 322-2404, 800-669-1069). Connected to Vista Grande (see below), with which it shares the distinction of having one of the highest occupancy rates in Palm Springs. Little wonder: the grounds, formerly a vacant lot, are a fantasyland of grottoes and waterfalls. Don't miss the tiki god with laser eyes. The 4 rooms are all different, but touches like halogen lamps, fully-stocked spice racks in the kitchens, and up-to-date furnishings make this a top choice. Reputation for high sexual content, but a place for couples, too. Rates: $135-$155.

Vista Grande (574 Warm Sands Dr, 322-2404, 800-669-1069). Attracts loyal clientele and frequent visits from those staying elsewhere, thanks in part to its two owners (Bob Mellen and Peter Tangel) and the fact that several pornos have been made here and at the small but lush Mirage resort next door. Kind of place where nude, below-the-waist photographs of past guests are prominently displayed. Above-average accommodations, beautiful plantings and a good-sized pool. Tends to be heavily-booked, so plan ahead. Rates: $79-$120.

The Villa (67-670 Carey Rd, Cathedral City, 328-7211). Once an Elizabeth Arden beauty farm. Today, the largest gay resort in Palm Springs (so large that a single person traveling alone might feel lost unless he's a good mixer) with 44 units, 2 1/2 acres of lush private grounds, but little else going for it. Popular with locals, who congregate around the pretty pool and sometimes cruise the grounds. Breakfast consists of coffee and cello-wrapped muffins. No VCRs. No nude sunbathing. Rates: $49-$105, depending on room type and season.

BUDGET CHOICE

Canyon Boys Club (960 N. Palm Canyon Dr, Palm Springs, 800-295-2582) is one of the larger properties in town, with 32 clean and modern motel-like rooms centered (some with kitchens and private patios) around the largest pool of any gay hotel here. Clothing optional. Grounds and location are nothing to fax home about, but if you're on a budget, then this is the place. Rates: $59-$79 all year round, $10 less Sun-Thur.

127

MOSTLY WOMEN

Delilah's Enclave (641 San Lorenzo Rd, 325-5269, 800-621-6973). Above-average furnishings, VCRs, buffet breakfast and lunch, and pretty grounds. Friendly management. Key differentiator: Well-mannered pets accepted. Good value. Rates: $50-$98.

SEE/DO

TEN THINGS NO SELF-RESPECTING GAY PERSON SHOULD MISS

The Joshua Tree National Monument (74485 National Monument Drive, Twentynine Palms, 619-367-7511, open 8 am to 4:30 pm, $5 admission). A don't-miss for nature lovers.

The McCallum Adobe (221 S. Palm Canyon Dr, 323-8297). Oldest remaining building in PS, built in 1885 for John McCallum, the first permanent white settler. Today it serves as the Historical Society's Museum and headquarters.

The Living Desert Museum (47-900 Portola Ave, Palm Desert 346-5694). Contains flora and fauna found in the Colorado Desert and in other arid climates.

The Agua Caliente Cultural Museum (219 S. Palm Canyon, Palm Springs, 323-0151). There's a museum store and exhibits detailing the lore and culture of the Agua Caliente band of Cahuilla Indians.

Village Fest is an evening street fair that takes place every Thu from 6 to 10 pm, providing some of the best shopping in Palm Springs.

Oasis Water Resort (1500 Gene Autry Trail, PS, 325-7873). Large water park with nine slides and a wave-action pool for body surfing. Okay, it's a bit mainstream, but on a hot day you might find it refreshing. There's also a small but uncrowded fitness center.

Palm Springs Aerial Tramway (Tramway Rd, off Highway 111, 325-1391). First opened to the public in 1963 and has been hauling skiers, hikers, and joyriders up Mt. San Jacinto ever since. Cross country ski rentals available Nov 15-Apr 15.

128

Fabulous Palm Springs Follies. In the same Plaza Theater from which Jack Benny broadcast during World War II, former vaudevillians and showgirls—some great-grandmothers—play ten shows a week to sold-out audiences.

Desert Adventures Jeep Tours (38225 South Palm Canyon Drive, 864-6530). Prices begin at $29 via Jeep, or $5 for just a walking tour.

The Palm Springs Municipal Swimming Pool. Huge and usually uncrowded. Great way to cool off, and it's free.

SPECIAL EVENTS

The Valley's **gay pride march** happens every Memorial Day weekend. The **Dinah Shore golf week** attracts lesbians every March. Every Easter weekend, a **White Party** draws 20,000 hunky men, from Southern California and beyond, who manage to make the natives feel physically inadequate. The **gay rodeo** comes to town the first weekend in November.

THE ROUTINE

Unlike Provincetown and Fire Island, there is no daily ritual here. On Sun, though, the party-faithful start at CC Construction for drinks and dancing from about 4-8, then move on to Spurs for C&W dancing.

KEEP FIT/RECREATION

Gold's Gym (4070 Airport Center Dr, 322-4653). Well-equipped but always-crowded near the airport. Day fee: $13, free if you belong to

Gold's elsewhere.

Palm Springs Athletic Club (543 S. Palm Canyon Dr, Palm Springs, 323-7722). Relatively new gay-owned gym within walking distance of downtown's bars and attractions. Mixed gay/straight clientele. Day fee: $10.

EAT

This is the land of the early-bird special, not fabulous late-night dining. Many restaurants close at 10 or 11 pm, even on Sat night. And don't expect five-star cuisine. Unlike Key West and South Beach, though, there *are* a lot of exclusively-gay dining spots, where you can feel totally comfortable.

TRES GAY

Choices Bar & Grill (36-815 Cathedral Canyon Dr, Cathedral City, 770-1290). Restaurant, bar, and pool hall in one. Inexpensive dishes that you order at the bar, and a "rain room" with thunder and lightning effects. Different. Entrees: $6-$11.

Flamingo Bar & Grill (233 E. Saturnino Rd, 325-4948). Gourmet pizzas. Chef from LA puts out incredible food. Entrees: $8-$16.

Shame on the Moon (69-950 Frank Sinatra Dr, Rancho Mirage, 324-5515). Gay-owned, attracts gay men of all ages, and is the best of the gay-frequented restaurants. Starters like ravioli in a basil cream sauce and a French brie quesadilla are tempting beginnings; chicken and broccoli pasta is a favorite, as is the angel hair pasta tossed with shrimp, artichoke hearts, and red peppers in olive oil and garlic. Entrees: $12-$18.

Two Gloria's (2400 N. Palm Canyon, 322-3224). New entrant by Gloria Greene. Should be popular with the more mature set. Entrees like pot roast, fried chicken. Entrees: $6-$12.

GAY FRIENDLY

The Red Pepper's (36-650 N. Sun Air Plaza, Cathedral City, 770-7007). The welcoming gay owner is justifiably proud of his food and prices. Above-average Mexican fare includes tostadas and enchiladas. Best thing on the menu is probably the chicken fajita. Exemplary service by people who are really glad to be here, and fabulous $3.95 margaritas. Entrees: $4-$10.

The Wilde Goose (67938 Highway 111, Cathedral City, 328-5775). Didn't have much of a gay crowd on our visit, although it is gay-friendly.

But the duck, prepared six different ways, is superb, as is the service. Entrees: $10-$25.

CHEAP EATS

Michael's Cafe (68-665 Highway 111, Cathedral City, 321-7197). The 1950's decor at this breakfast and lunch joint is original, not retro, Eisenhower period; gay men share the place with seniors who know a bargain when they see one. Entrees: under $8.

The Rainbow Cactus (212 S. Indian Canyon, Palm Springs, 325-3868). Attracts an older gay crowd. Low prices, and although the lunch and dinner menus are nothing to write home about, as one patron put it, "At these prices, you don't have one goddamn reason to complain." Even better: a pianist often serenades diners at night. Entrees: around $6.

Richard's Restaurant (68-599 Highway 111, Cathedral City, 321-2841). Basically a steak and potatoes place, with a small but competent menu. Stay away from any fish offerings (this is the desert), and stick to the meat and chicken entrees. A lively, more mature crowd frequents the bar; a pianist adds charm to this cozy spot. Entrees: $6-$16.

PLAY/MEET

Whereas Key West and South Beach only have a handful of gay bars each, Palm Springs boasts nearly a dozen. What's going on here? Some of these places serve as hobbies for semi-retired entrepreneurs who don't need to make it all work financially. Different venues are popular on different nights, and some are dead except on the weekend.

MOSTLY FOR DANCING

C. C. Construction (68-449 Perez Road, Cathedral City, 324-4241). Popular on Sun afternoons, when C&W music is on tap.

Choices (68-352 Perez Rd, Cathedral City, 321-1145). Housed in an erstwhile warehouse, this is a large space divided in two: one area is a high tech cabaret, featuring nationally-recognized talent (I saw gay comedian Michael Greer bring the Mona Lisa to life in an unforgettably manic performance). Patrons sit around little tables with fairy lamps on them. The other side is a classic disco with a good sound and light system. Upstairs is a glass-enclosed viewing gallery from which you can watch the go-go boys go go go.

MOSTLY FOR DRINKING/CRUISING

Delilah's (68-657 Palm Canyon, Cathedral City, 324-3268). Next door to Michael's Cafe (see under **Eat**), and the desert's only video bar—primarily for women. Thu to Sun.

Streetbar (224 E. Arenas Rd, 320-1266). Neighborhood place with friendly bartenders and patrons. Within walking distance of the Warm Sands area.

Spurs Saloon (36737 Cathedral Canyon, Cathedral City, 619-321-1233). Country & Western music, two-stepping, line dancing lessons, men in 10 gallon hats, rodeo videos on the big screen TV. A small cover charge buys your first drink. Friendly crowd and owner, who will buy a drink for any newcomer.

131

LEATHER

The Tool Shed (600 E. Sunny Dunes Rd, 320-3299). Makes a brave attempt to be leather-scary, with its chains and graffiti-scrawled walls. Two rooms, pool table, amiable crowd.

Wolfs (67-625 Highway 111, Cathedral City, 321-9688). Small leather bar.

SHOP

Palm Springs doesn't have much in the way of world-class shopping.

Paper Lilli (191 S. Palm Canyon Dr, 327-3373). Selection of unusual cards and gifts.

R&R Menswear (333 N. Palm Canyon Dr, 320-3007). Don't expect the range of hip fashions you'd find in South Beach, but useful for pool togs and other clothing.

Desert Fashion Plaza (Palm Canyon Dr, 320-8282). The main mall, with all the usual stores, anchored by a Saks.

RESOURCES

GAY/HIV INFORMATION

Desert AIDS Project (750 Vella Rd, Palm Springs, 323-2118). Provides free testing and other services.

Desert Women's Association (363-7565). Lesbian group.

GENERAL INFORMATION

The **Palm Springs Gay Tourism Council** (PO Box 2885, PS 92263). Provides general gay information.

BOOKSTORE

As of this writing, there is no all-gay bookstore in the area. **Crown Books** has a good selection of gay titles, although not in a special section. Rumors come and go that someone will open a store, and you'd think that a population base of 250,000 could support one (Provincetown has one, with 7,000 year-rounders).

PUBLICATIONS

The Bottom Line (323-0552). Published weekly.

Desert Community Directory (available by sending $1.50 to PO Box 9325, PS, CA 92263). The local gay yellow pages, twice yearly.

MegaScene (327-5178). Appears bimonthly.

PROVINCETOWN, MA

AREA CODE 508

WHAT TO EXPECT

When you think about it, it's interesting how many gay and lesbian areas lie in splendid isolation. Provincetown, Key West, Palm Springs—they're all in the middle of nowhere or at the ends of the earth. Even San Francisco lies at the end of continent.

Provincetown (don't immediately brand yourself as a tourist by calling it P-town) is unique in that it's literally at the end of the earth (the earth in this case being Cape Cod) and, in addition, it's an honest-to-God working fishing village and artist colony, surrounded by some of the country's best beaches and some beautiful nature preserves. But it's also a year-round gay and lesbian community, and gay and straight seem to get along well.

Even in the dead of winter, Provincetown is a lively place. More and more, people are choosing to live here year round, and only in January and early February, roughly the period just after New Year's and just before Valentine's Day, do people start talking to the furniture. Many weekenders now spend Halloween, Thanksgiving, Christmas, New Year's, Valentine's Day, and other minor holidays here. Another trend: over the last few years, Provincetown has become increasingly more lesbian-oriented.

Like Janus, the Roman god of gates and doorways, Provincetown has two faces: there's the honky-tonk hustle and bustle, the clubs and after-hours parties; and then there's the quieter, contemplative aspect nurtured by the surrounding National Seashore. Unlike Fire Island, there's a lot more to do here than beach and party. But if this is your first visit, you might want to experience the whole drill.

Provincetown's crazed summer routine, with the continual parade down Commercial Street and more costume changes than the Christmas show at Radio City, doesn't thrill everyone. Now and then visitors will carp, "Oh, Provincetown, how can you stand the noise and the crowds?" Indeed, the schedule can be rigorous. Line up for breakfast, trek off to the beach, shower and change for Tea Dance, "after tea" at the Pied, new outfit, dinner, more dancing, the scene at Spiritus, after-hours parties—interspersed with shopping and people watching.

In fact, though, Provincetown's honky tonk side is confined to the high rent district along Commercial Street, reaching its apogee in a garishly-decorated T-shirt and bumper sticker emporium called Shop

Therapy. But even in the bustling summer season, you can leave the hubbub and discover natural and man-made wonders just minutes away. Truth is, one can spend a long week end, or even a week, and never come within sniffing distance of a fried dough shop.

BEST TIME TO COME

Every season has its charms, even winter. But to appreciate the scene, come between Memorial and Labor Day. Many people think late September is optimal.

GETTING THERE

134

You can drive from Boston by taking the Southeast Expressway (I-93) south to Route 3 and then to Route 6. A warning, though: The police in Eastham and Truro, whose territory you cross, have nothing better to do than stop cars, even for minor offenses. *Strictly* observe all motor vehicle regulations—including posted speeds, missing tail lights, registration, and inspection stickers. From Memorial Day onward, there's ferry service from Boston on Bay State Cruises (617-723-7800). Trip time is 2 1/2 hours. The easiest and most dramatic way to go is to fly on Cape Air (800-352-0714). The flight takes 25 minutes.

GETTING AROUND

You probably won't need a car here. Bikes are a good idea, though. Taxi service is available to get you from the airport to town.

STAY

Over the past few years, a younger generation of guest house owners has taken over; these folks don't flee to Florida at the first sign of cold weather, so more and more places are open year round. There are nearly 70 gay or gay-friendly inns and B&B's catering to men; and over a dozen for women. Note: **Provincetown Reservations System** (800-648-0364) is a central clearing house for most B&B's.

MOSTLY GAY

The Anchor Inn (175 Commercial St, 487-0432). Right on the water. Wonderful old New England seacoast lobby, 24 units all with private bath, color TV, deck or other outside space; most with direct ocean views. Built in 1912 as a private home for a fishing captain. Ultra-modern furniture is in good condition but doesn't really fit the old New England architecture. Rates: $85-$135.

The Beaconlite (12 Winthrop St, 487-9603). One of the best B&B's in town. Ten attractive rooms, all with private baths, TVs. Rates: $50-$120 off season to $75-$145 in the summer. A 2BR house sleeping up to six with large fireplace and yard goes for $110-$150.

The Boatslip (161 Commercial St, 487-1669). Popular and noisy; clean and comfortable, the 45-room motel-like 'Slip is right on the water (all rooms have views). There's a pool that gets a lot of action during the day, and the famous tea dances are held here in the afternoons. Rates: $110-$150 peak season, $85-$100 June, $75-$90 fall, $60-$80 spring.

Brass Key (9 Court St, 487-9005, 800-842-9858). The most luxurious gay B&B in town. Owned by the same people who run the Key West version, it offers turn down service, A/C, TV, VCR, and direct dial phones in all 12 rooms, two of which have a fireplace. All have private baths. Continental breakfast and summer cocktail hour, tape library, and free parking are other reasons to stay. Rates: $60-$175 off season, and $155-$220 high season.

135

The Fairbanks Inn (90 Bradford St, 487-0386). Lesbian-owned but mixed clientele. Sixteen adorable rooms, 10 with fireplaces and reproduction antiques. No private baths with first floor rooms, some on second floor. A few rooms with kitchens and private access. Best rooms: 3 and 4. Rates: summer and holidays $65-$120 (apartments sleeping 4 $145-$175); off season $35-$100.

The Gifford House (9-11 Carver St, 487-0688). Under new management, a Provincetown institution: historic, multi-storied building with an inviting lobby and an adjacent bar and disco. On warm summer evenings, the lobby and Porch Bar used to be jammed with good looking and friendly patrons. The new owners are trying to revive that scene. Cabaret room showcases entertainment such as The Ten Percent Revue. With all this activity, not a place for the early-to-bed crowd. Closes for season early Nov. Rates: $39-$72 off-season; $66-$120 in.

Lands End Inn (15 Commercial St, 487-0706). The most offbeat place in town, an old curiosity shop run amok with Tiffany lamps and a most unusual collection of vases, all perched on a hill with mesmerizing ocean views. Clientele not especially gay. Rates: $87-$175 off, $98-$250 in season.

Red Inn (15 Commercial St, 487-0050). Built in 1805, four recently-redone rooms; probably the town's most quaint, coziest lodging. Easy walk to the beach, but far from downtown; good restaurant. Rates: $75 off, $125-$150 summer.

Six Webster Place (6 Webster Pl, 487-2266). Ten attractive rooms with antiques, working fireplaces, crooked wide-plank floors. Pleasant management. Rates: $50-$95, depending on day of week/time of year and whether shared or private bath.

MOSTLY FOR LESBIANS

Bradford Gardens Inn (178 Bradford St, 487-1616). Delightful with gleaming wood floors and Laura Ashley-esque wallpapers. Try to get one of the eight rooms in the main house (eight other units are in adjacent cottages). Mixed clientele: mostly lesbian and straight couples. Rates: $99-$109 off season, $116-$129 summer.

Plums B&B (160 Bradford St, 487-3203). Women only. Nice antiques and private baths, terrific owner. But don't stay here if you have an aversion to purple. Rates: $78 off-season, $95 summer.

PET-FRIENDLY

White Wind Inn (174 Commercial St, 486-1526). 11 rooms, all bright and freshly painted with soft wool Berber carpeting. Some with four-poster beds, most with VCR or cable TV, two with working fireplaces. Rates: $80 off-season, $125 summer.

SEE/DO

TEN THINGS NO SELF-RESPECTING GAY PERSON SHOULD MISS

Tea Dance at the Boat Slip (487-1669). A Provincetown institution. Even if you're not a party type, do it at least once.

The Pilgrim Monument and Provincetown Museum (487-1310). Great views from the top of the country's tallest all-granite structure. In the museum, ask about Steve Bonnett, a reputedly-gay pirate captain whose ship was named *The Revenge.*

Cape Cod National Seashore's Bicycle Trails. Over five miles of adventure. Rent a bike at gay owned **Tim's Cycle Shop** (306 Commercial St, 487-6628).

Spiritus, 1 am. At least one night, stay up late to catch the scene outside this popular pizza parlor. Boy meets boy meets boy meets....

Self-guided walking tours. Maps are available from bookstores and gift shops. Most of the sights are along Commercial St.

Sunset whale watch cruise. Offered by the Dolphin Fleet (offices located in the Chamber of Commerce Building at the head of the Provincetown Pier, 800-826-9300 in Mass.) or the Portuguese Princess (487-2651).

Beech Forest. National Park Service walking trails showcasing Provincetown's natural landscape.

Art's Dune Tours (487-1950). Eco-sensitive four-wheeling through the dunes is much more fun than it sounds.

National Seashore Visitors Center (Race Point Road, 487-1256). Free ranger-led hikes through the Seashore's flora, fauna, and history.

Get a beach fire permit. Rangers give them out first come first served—call 487-1256 up to three days in advance. Just before sunset, snuggle with someone special on Race Point Beach and have a romantic cookout as the sun sinks into the Atlantic (trust me, you'll be facing west).

137

THE ROUTINE

Every gay beach resort has a drill, and Provincetown is no exception. It begins each day with breakfast around 10 am. Then it's off to the beach until 2:30 or so, when *le tout Provincetown* trudges back to guest house or condo for a nap, shower, and costume change. Tea Dance at the **Boat Slip** (161 Commercial St) comes next (4-6 pm), followed by After-Tea at the **Pied Piper** just down the street (a mostly-girls place, but popular with men during these hours). Around 8, it's back for another shower and possibly a fashion makeover, then dinner around 9. From there it's the A (for Atlantic) House, Back Street (at the Gifford House), or the Pied (women only now) for drinks and dancing. Still standing? At 1 am, when bars close, everyone gathers at **Spiritus,** the Commercial Street pizza legend, where they hang out on the sidewalk (often blocking whatever traffic there is) desperately looking for Mr. Right. For the hardy and well-connected, invitation-only after-hours parties often follow; Spiritus is a good place to find out about them.

KEEP FIT/RECREATION

Mussel Beach (56 Shankpainter Rd, near the A&P, 487-0001). The best place to work out. Bright, clean equipment, including Stairmasters and Lifecycles. Day passes are $8; seasonal/yearly memberships also available.

SPECIAL EVENTS

Carnival Week. Held in mid-August, sponsored by the Provincetown Business Guild, the gay chamber of commerce (487-2313).

EAT

There are many good restaurants here, most featuring freshly-caught seafood. But eating in Provincetown, especially in the peak summer months, can be a problem. First, there are few great restaurants—wonderful standouts that would be huge successes in a major city. That may seem rather harsh and arbitrary, but it's the result of ten years of eating. Second, eateries get crowded and many don't take (or don't honor) reservations. No matter where you go, you'll find a gay/straight mix, but all are gay-friendly. Having said that, there's a wide choice, and you'll enjoy yourself.

Here are some favorites:

GAY FRIENDLY

Front Street (230 Commercial St, 487-9715). In a brick-walled Victorian basement, menu changes weekly although rack of lamb and duck are constants. Entrees: $17-$25.

The Lobster Pot (321 Commercial St, 487-0842). Provincetown institution where it's impossible to get a bad meal. But it's not particularly gay. Entrees like tuna and scallops shitake range from $14-$19.

The Martin House (157 Commercial St, 487-1327). The most romantic place in town, a gay-owned restaurant situated in an authentic 18th century home (ask for a table on the ground floor, next to a fireplace if one is roaring). Entrees like sesame crusted tuna on soba noodles range between $12-22.

The Mews (429 Commercial St, 487-1500). Rack of lamb and bouillabaisse are excellent. Entrees: $14-$20.

Napi's (7 Freeman St, 487-1145). A year-round stand-by featuring fresh ingredients and a huge menu. Service can be slow, especially in winter when it's one of the few games in town. Entrees: $11-$20.

The Red Inn (15 Commercial St, 487-0050). A bit expensive, but the setting is special with great water views. Best bet: Red Inn baked stuffed lobster. Entrees: $19-24.

CHEAP EATS

Café Blasé (328 Commercial, 487-9465). Eat lunch at least once at this outdoor eatery with decent hamburgers and salads and the best people watching in town. Most things under $10.

Spiritus Pizza (190 Commercial St, 487-2808). Always useful for a slice after the beach, but the real action happens at 1 am, when the bars close and hundreds of hungry (in all senses) gay men congregate out front.

PLAY/MEET

The Atlantic House (8 Masonic St, 487-3821). Built between 1798 and 1812, and formerly a hotel that provided lodging to such luminaries as Eugene O'Neill and Tennessee Williams, now a popular bar and disco. Rustic decor—nothing high-tech here. Operates year round; crowded on major holiday weekends, even during off-season.

Backstreet (9-11 Carver, 487-0688). Part of the Gifford House complex. Popular, low-ceilinged dance club, somewhat claustrophobic. The adjacent **Porch Bar** used to be exceptionally popular, but has fallen out of favor recently.

The Boatslip (161 Commercial St, 800-451-SLIP). The most happening spot from 4-6:30 pm. Large outdoor deck; small, packed, fun dance floor inside. Evening dancing less popular.

The Crown & Anchor (247 Commercial, 487-1430). Cabaret shows, dancing, outdoor space. Not as happening as Backstreet, the A-House, and the Boat Slip tea dances.

Kitty's (67 Shankpainter Rd, 487-8320). Dance club in a somewhat remote location across from the A&P, popular Fri and Sat night.

The Pied Piper (193A Commercial, 487-1527). A women's dance club with outdoor decks. Where everyone goes after the Boat Slip.

SHOP

About 200 one-of-a-kind boutiques line Commercial St. The town fathers are steadfastly against chains and have banned Burger King and McDonald's, although they did permit a Benetton's outlet store to open.

BodyBody (295 and 315 Commercial St, 487-2751). The first location is for women, the second for men. Both offer comfortable body-conscious casual wear with flair.

Cape Card (230 Commercial St, 487-2029). Witty and x-rated cards, postcards, souvenirs.

Mad Hatter (360 Commercial St, 487-4063). Clever selection of reasonably priced headgear for men and women.

No. 5 (199 Commercial St, 487-1594). Italian imports, Issey Miyake, Calvin Klein, and other upmarket clothes for men and women.

Zeus (169 Commercial, 487-2501). Decorative arts and potpourri oil (the pina colada is terrific).

RESOURCES

GENERAL INFORMATION

Provincetown Business Guild (the gay chamber of commerce): 800-637-8696

GAY/HIV INFORMATION

Provincetown AIDS Support Group (487-9445).

BOOKSTORES

Now Voyager (357 Commercial, 487-0848). Newer and carries more beach reading. Friendly place to ask about what's happening.

Provincetown Bookshop (246 Commercial Street, 487-0964). Small but intelligent selection.

Recovering Hearts Bookstore (4 Standish St, 487-4875). Specializes in self-help and women's titles.

PUBLICATIONS

The Provincetown *Advocate* is the old standby newspaper. There is no year-round gay paper, but the Boston papers put out special Provincetown editions during the summer.

RUSSIAN RIVER, CA

AREA CODE 707

WHAT TO EXPECT

No Russians live on the Russian River, but the area got its name from a scouting party of Russian fur traders who landed ten miles west of here at Bodega Bay in search of a food source to supply their Aleutian outposts. Today, the Russian River area is Boston's Provincetown or Washington's Rehoboth Beach, except that it's hard to imagine someone coming here from far away to spend an entire week (whereas you could easily do that in Provincetown). There's just not that much to do, unless, of course, you're a confirmed oenophile, in which case the nearby wineries of Sonoma will keep you more than occupied. Certainly, if you're already in San Francisco and it's summer then this rustic area, just 90 minutes from Fog City, is worth a detour.

Maybe half of the residents are gay here (it's easy to be open about it). There's a small town feeling and the residents prefer the slower pace. In Jan and Mar of 1995, the river overflowed its banks, causing massive destruction. The good news is that millions of dollars of insurance money have spawned widespread renovation. Most places should be open by the time you read this.

The sleepy little town of Guerneville forms the nucleus of the Russian River and consists basically of one main street with a cluster of shops and restaurants. Everything looks as if time had passed it by. The original "Rexall" sign on the drugstore hasn't been changed in 50 years; there's an old "Esso" sign on a gas station outside of town. It's like "Back to the Future." But who cares? When the fog rolls in from the ocean and drifts over the tops of the towering pine trees poking their way into the blue sky, it's magic.

BEST TIME TO COME

Anytime but winter.

GETTING THERE

From San Francisco, take 101 north to Russian River Resort exit, which leads into Guerneville.

GETTING AROUND

You'll need a car, especially to visit local wineries.

STAY

All addresses are in Guerneville unless otherwise noted.

GAY

Avalon Inn (4th and Mill, 800-994-9566 or 869-9566). Next door to Triple R Resort (see below), 18 units, fresh-looking decor, new owners, ask for a redecorated room. Cruisy atmosphere on busy weekends. Grounds need further beautification. Rates: $50-$115.

Fife's (16467 River Rd, 869-0656). Pretty much the nerve center for gay activities, with 49 units on 15 acres with towering redwoods and colorful hydrangeas. Full restaurant and bar, heated pool with nude sunbathing. Units 302-316 are best; 302 has a private deck, nice carpeting. Rates: $50-$100.

Highlands Resort (14000 Woodland Dr, 869-0333). Rooms overlooking pool very popular, as are cabins, which offer kitchen units. Camping on grounds. 99.9% gay. Nice lounge, quiet, no bar or restaurant. Five min. walk from downtown but seems like you're in the middle of the redwoods. Nude sunbathing. Rates: $45-$105.

Paradise Cove (14711 Armstrong Woods Rd, 800-880-2706, 869-2706). Fifteen stylish rooms, some with fireplaces, platform beds, private decks for nude sunbathing. Rates: $65-$135.

Triple R Resort (a.k.a. Russian River Resort, 4th & Mill Sts, 869-0691). The most sexually frisky place in town. Cable TV but no phones, walking distance to everything, pool and hot tub, mixed-age crowd. Excellent restaurant. Rates: $40-$90.

Willows (15905 River Rd). Thirteen rooms (9 with private bath) on 5 peaceful acres (room 4 has nice views). Some rooms subject to road noise. Breakfast included Rates: $49-$109.

The Woods (16881 Armstrong Woods Rd, 869-0260). Simple, dark, modern cabins some with working fireplaces, gray carpets, wood ceilings. Peaceful grounds, smell of pine, grass. Volleyball courts, two nice pools, one clothing optional. Restaurant serves breakfast and brunch on the weekend. Motel rooms sell out first. Rates: $50-$120.

GAY-FRIENDLY

Applewood (13555 Highway 116, Pocket Canyon, 869-9093 or 800-226-APPLE). Gay-owned 16-room romantic hideaway with mostly-straight clientele—the most luxurious accommodations in the area. Down comforters, fireplaced sitting rooms, beautiful grounds, exceptional restaurant. Rates: $125-$250.

143

Highland Dell Inn (21050 River Blvd, Monte Rio, 865-1759). Gay-owned charmer on river near Village Inn (see below). Knotty pine, Victorian antiques, gingerbread balustrades. Ten rooms, 8 with private bath. About 40% gay clientele but rising. Dinner served Sat only: $22-$35 for 5 courses. Rates: $56-$225.

Huckleberry Springs (PO Box 400, Monte Rio, 800-822-2683, 865-2683). Sixty-acre mountain-top retreat, definitely the most unusual lodgings in the area. At the end of a seemingly endless single lane road that keeps on going up, four comfortable cabins done in California Country style with fireplaces but no TVs or phones. Includes breakfast and dinner. Mixed clientele. Rates: $175 for two, $75 each extra person.

Rio Villa Beach Resort (20292 Hwy 116, Monte Rio, 865-1143). Gay-owned, but mostly straight clientele (50% gay on major holiday weekends). Rates: $115-$150.

The Village Inn (20822 River Blvd, Monte Rio, 865-2304). Even though it's only about 50% gay and not within walking distance of anything, this charming country inn is where I'd stay. Scenes from "Holiday Inn" (Bing Crosby, White Christmas) were filmed here; good place to bring your parents. Antiques, fresh decor, river views, 18 units, some with shared baths. Built in 1906, family-owned. Rates: $30-$130.

SEE/DO

TEN THINGS NO SELF-RESPECTING GAY PERSON SHOULD MISS

Armstrong Woods. Hike the redwoods. Trails run from under a mile to over ten.

Gay Pride Festival. Happens in early June. Contact Chamber of Commerce for details.

Annual River's Cup Canoe Race and Anything that Floats Regatta. A bit like the river raft race held during Hotlanta in Atlanta. A bit. Usually takes place in early Aug.

Wine tours. The Chamber of Commerce has maps to guide you through the vineyards.

Horseback riding. Armstrong Woods Pack Station (887-2939) offers gentle steeds.

Go Canoeing on the river. Burke's Canoe Trips (887-1222) will equip you.

Rent a bike. Mike's Bike Rental has mountain bikes for $23/day (869-1106).

River Rep Theater (865-2905). See La Cage aux Folles or similar plays here.

Drive along the Pacific Coast. Via Route 1 in the Bodega Bay area.

Tour Fort Ross State Park, restored site of an 1812 Russian settlement ("Ross" is derived from the word "Russia").

SPECIAL EVENTS

Russian River Rodeo (mid Jun).

Russian River Jazz Festival (mid Sep, 869-3940).

EAT

TOP TABLES

Applewood (13555 Highway 116, Pocket Canyon, 869-9093). Sensational set menu with items like herb-crusted rack of lamb and Tuscan roast chicken. Four courses: about $32.

TRES GAY

Fife's Restaurant (16467 River Rd, 869-0656). Small, basic menu with items like charbroiled lamb chops. Entrees: $12-$16.

Lalita's Cantina (16225 Main St, 869-3238). Mexican cuisine, live entertainment, lesbian owned. Entrees: everything under $9.

GAY FRIENDLY

Sweet's (16251 Main St, 869-3383). New gay owners, brand new decor. Specials like mussels steamed in vermouth with garlic and roasted red peppers. Entrees: $8-$16.

Village Inn (20822 River Blvd, Monte Rio, 865-2304). Fare such as blackened red snapper, lime chicken, and filet mignon. Entrees: $9-$17.

145

CHEAP EATS

Breeze Inn Bar-B-Q (15640 River Rd, 869-9208). Probably the best place to eat in town; excellent ribs and smoked salmon, named best BBQ in Northern CA. Entrees: $4-$19.

Brew Moon (16248 Main St, 869-0201). Lesbian-owned store-front coffee house with live entertainment Tue, Thu, and Sat.

PLAY/MEET

MOSTLY FOR DANCING

The Jungle (16135 Main St, 869-1400). Pretty much it when it comes to dancing. Former theater turned into a disco. Large, well-designed space.

MOSTLY FOR DRINKING/CRUISING

Molly Brown's (14120 Old Cazadero Rd, 869-0511). Old road house with neon beer signs in the windows. Also a restaurant.

Rainbow Cattle Company (16220 Main St, 869-0206). Friendly, rustic bar.

SHOP

River Mist Antiques (16359 Main, 869-9707). Antiques, crafts, gifts.

Up the River (16212 Main St, 869-3167). Menswear, "Pride" items, cards and gifts.

RESOURCES

GENERAL INFORMATION

Russian River Chamber of Commerce (16200 First St, PO Box 331, Guerneville 95446, 869-9000).

GAY INFORMATION

Russian River Gay and Lesbian Business Assn (869-GLBA).

SOUTH BEACH, FL

AREA CODE 305

WHAT TO EXPECT

South Beach lies at the southern end of an island city—Miami Beach, Florida. (As usual, we vacation in the middle of a desert, at the end of something, or on an island). For our purposes, the epicenter of SoBe, as it has come to be called, is the pastel kitsch Art Deco District, a one-square-mile collection of 800 historic buildings bordered north to south by 6th and 23rd streets, and east to west by the Atlantic Ocean and Lenox Avenue. Recently, South Beach has become the darling of fashion photographers and other hipsters. But it was the gay settlers who revived this town from its near-death experience. Now, reading the gay press, you'd think that the city of Miami Beach was a gay republic, filled only with beautiful gays and lesbians. In reality, there are plenty of straights here (although many of them are beautiful, too, in part because they've pretty much taken over the gay look). You'll also find plenty of old people, although they've been relocated (in some cases, in an offhand manner). Such urban ills as dirt, crime, and, as of this writing at least, lots of deserted, unrehabilitated buildings number among SoBe's less attractive attributes. Although much renewal has taken place, some streets still vacillate between fashionable and faded.

But who cares. The people are all gorgeous, with to-die-for bodies. Several times during my visit I literally stopped in my tracks to turn around and gawk at some passing god. How can you not gape at the ponytailed hunks with shaven, tanned, perfectly bulging pectorals and dainty earrings gliding by on roller-skates, skateboards, or bicycles—nearly knocking over, as they zoom by, elderly ladies negotiating their walkers. Yes, pecs, pecs, pecs. Pecs on skateboards. Pecs on Rollerblades. Pecs on bikes. Pecs playing volleyball. Pecs just plain walking around.

Now that Mainstream America is coming back to South Beach, one wonders what will happen to the gays. I spoke about South Beach past and future with Jim Balazano, a charming transplanted Bostonian who works as an openly gay elementary school teacher. "People are cautious about making friends because everyone's so transient here. They leave when something better comes up," he told me. "The gay population invaded South Beach and reinvigorated it. The difference between Boston and South Beach? South Beach is a party town trying to be a community. Boston is a community trying to be a party town. What's happened here is like what happened in the South End. Gays go into a place no one else wants to live, renovate, it becomes popular with upscale straights, the people who made it hip can't afford it any more as rents go up, and then the gays move on. That will happen here, too. It's already happening."

BEST TIME TO COME

South Beach is rapidly becoming a year-round destination, but winter makes the most sense.

GETTING THERE

Fly into Miami International Airport. Don't bother renting a car at the airport. Instead, take Super Shuttle, a van service, for about $10 per person; a taxi will cost $25-$30. The ride takes about 30 minutes. If you need a car for an onward journey, pick it up in Miami Beach. Budget has an office at 22nd and Collins; Avis is at 21st and Collins.

GETTING AROUND

Parking and traffic can be a problem; you really don't need a car anyway. Walk, rollerblade, or rent a bike.

STAY

There are dozens of deco hotels that welcome gays, but just a few gay guest houses. If I had to choose one guest house, it would probably be The Jefferson House (see below). An easy way to book rooms is through **South Florida Hotel Network,** a gay-owned reservation service run by Bob Guilmartin, a local entrepreneur and South Beach pioneer (800-538-3616, fax 538-5858).

GAY GUEST HOUSES

The guest houses here are smaller than and lack the atmosphere and conviviality of those in Key West, but the owners provide a warm welcome. Perhaps because there's so much to do outside the guest house enclaves, they're not the focus of the gay experience.

The Bayliss (504 Fourteenth St, 534-0010). Owned by the two nicest people I met in South Beach (they also own the GW shop, see below). Not all rooms have private baths. Queen-bedded rooms comfortable and homey, with direct-dial phones. Rates $95-$100 high season, $65 low; an efficiency (with small kitchen) goes for $75 nightly, $350 weekly.

The Jefferson House (1018 Jefferson Ave, 534-5247). Run by a friendly and helpful former restaurateur. The clean, bright rooms offer private baths and are either in the main house, or in a small building in back. No in-room phones. Rates: $75-125 in season, $60-$105 off.

Normandy South (2474 Prairie Ave, 674-1197). Six-room, all-male, clothing optional, strict non-smoking policy. Large pool area. Well-decorated rooms with TVs and fridges, but no phones. Cont. breakfast. Rates: $90-$145 in season; $70-$110 off-season.

GAY HOTELS

Colours, The Mantell Guest Inn (255 W. 24th St, 531-3601 or 800-ARRIVAL). Opened late August 94. Former condo building with studio units. Large pool. Cont. breakfast/sunset cocktails. Almost all gay/lesbian. Rates: $49-$119 off season, $79-$159 in season.

Hotel Impala (1228 Collins Ave, 673-2021). Gay-owned and -operated, luxurious and elegant, boasts a central location. All 17 rooms offer TV, VCR, and CD players, voice mail, central air, large bathrooms, imported cotton linens and robes, and striking interior design. Suites have touches like portable phones, fridges, and wet bars. Rates: from $159-$185; suites begin at $225.

Raleigh (1775 Collins Ave, 800-848-1775). My favorite gay place to stay is this 107-room a deluxe hotel designed in 1940 by noted architect L. Murray Dixon and the only beach-front hotel that has been completely restored. Center piece: the huge, palm-fringed Busby Berkeley-style swimming pool, with its seriously-equipped outside gym, and 300 feet of white sand beach right in back. All rooms fully-gadgeted with VCRs, CD players, JVC radios, cassette tape players, and alarm clocks. The new owners retained some of the original deco touches, like the stainless steel Jetsonesque headboards. Rates: $139-$189 low season, $159-$209 high season.

GAY-FRIENDLY HOTELS

Gay guests will feel welcome almost anywhere, but especially at the following:

The Lily Guest House (835 Collins Ave, 535-9900). Relatively new, 18 studios and suites, well-renovated, sparkling wood floors, nice furniture, with kitchenettes. Mostly gay. Rates: $150-$250 in season, $100-$175 off season.

Marlin Hotel (1200 Collins, 673-8770 or 800-538-9076). Popular with designers, recording stars and other celebs. Aqua, lavender, pink, and tangerine interiors—splashed, sponged, and dribbled on like a Jackson Pollock. Lobby worth seeing even if you're not staying here, which you probably won't—reservations are as tight as a lifeguard's Speedo. Nice in-room touches like down comforters, kitchenettes, minibars, CD players and VCRs, and batik bathrobes. Rates: $200-$225.

The Park Central (640 Ocean Dr, 538-1611). Old deco hotel now lovingly restored. Rooms on the front face the ocean, but can be noisy. The restaurant is good, and the lobby great for people-watching. I joined in on a conversation between a hunky male model (straight, but very friendly) and his camera crew as they sat waiting for the light to improve. The topic: the deplorable restaurant service in South Beach. "There *is* no service," the model informed us. Rates: $60-$125 low season, $120-$165 high season.

SEE/DO

Sightseeing (other than the human kind) isn't really the point in Miami Beach. There are no major attractions in Miami Beach itself. You come here to soak in the sun on the beaches and people-watch in the cafés.

NINE THINGS NO SELF-RESPECTING GAY PERSON SHOULD MISS

Official Art Deco District Walking Tour. Led by local historians and preservationists, this 90-minute walk concentrates on Ocean Dr and Collins Ave, and leaves every Sat at 10:30 am from the Miami Design Preservation League's Art Deco Welcome Center, at the Ocean Front Auditorium (1001 Ocean Dr, 672-2014).

Boy-watch. Bring a camera with a telephoto lens.

Tea dance at Amnesia (see under **Play/Meet**).

Rent a pair of Rollerblades (South Beach Skates, 534-2252) or a bike (Cycles on the Beach, 713 Fifth St, 673-2055) along the beach or bring your own.

The New World Symphony (555 Lincoln Rd, 673-3331). Performs between Oct and Apr.

Coconut Grove Playhouse (3500 Main Highway, Coconut Grove, 442-4000). Stages innovative productions between Oct and Jun.

The Ballet Theatre of Miami (442-4840). Performs in South Beach on occasion, as does the **Miami Ballet Company** (667-5985).

Gay and lesbian beach (12th and Ocean).

Colony Theater (674-1040). Catch a gay comic here.

THE ROUTINE

Like Provincetown and Fire Island, but unlike Key West, the daily routine centers around the beach here. Get up, breakfast, go to beach around 11 am. Stay until three or four. Refresh at an Ocean Drive café. Shower and nap. Dine around 9. Clubs don't start to get crowded until 11 pm, and many go strong until 5 in the morning, even though alcohol isn't served past 2 am.

KEEP FIT/RECREATION

Body Tech (1253 Washington Ave, 674-8222). At 2800 square feet, by far the biggest fitness center; caters to a largely gay clientele. Day fee: $13.

151

Idol's Gym (1000 Lincoln Road, 532-0089). Smaller, but clean and almost exclusively gay. Day fee: $10.

SPECIAL EVENTS

South Beach is famous for its large beach parties, often with very hefty ad-mission prices—but proceeds usually go to charity. A **Winter Party** is held in Feb. Call the Business Guild (see **Gay Information**) for exact dates.

EAT

Restaurants, restaurants everywhere—the eating here is better than in just about any other gay resort. But there are no eateries where you'll be guaranteed a mostly-gay clientele, if that's what you're looking for. Still, you can steal a kiss just about anywhere. Warning: many restaurants add a 15% tip automatically, which may explain the lackluster service for which South Beach is infamous—that and the fact that, after all, your waiter doesn't really want to be a waiter; he's really a model between assignments, and could be off to Milan tomorrow if the call comes. So chill.

TOP TABLES

Bang (1516 Washington Ave, 531-2361). Loved it. Tin-ceilinged, high-energy, contemporary American menu. Typical entree: oak-roasted whole Florida snapper with Thai spiced noodles. Robbin Haas is the chef. Entrees: $7.50-$18.

Pacific Time (915 Lincoln Rd, 534-5979). Tops most best-restaurant lists thanks to its innovative Pacific Rim-inspired chow. Entrees in the $16-$20 range.

Pappamondo (1342 Washington Ave, 673-1265). A winner. Northern Italian spot with a European, casual atmosphere and excellent service—a rare commodity in SoBe. Emphasis here is on homemade pastas with lots of fresh herbs—everything is yummy. Entrees: $8-$21.

CHEAP EATS

11th Street Diner (11th St and Washington Ave, 534-6373). Used to live in Wilkes Barre, PA. Then it was restored and trucked to its present location. The food is strictly retro, as in Mom's Pot Roast and Southern Fried Chicken. The chocolate milkshakes were voted best in Miami. Entrees: $8-$11.

News Café (800 Ocean Dr, 538-6397). Service with attitude thicker than the Manhattan Yellow Pages. Nice little selection of books, magazines, and newspapers, though—useful for the *NY Times*. The good news at the News is that you can sit all day with a cup of coffee and watch the pretty world go by. Your waitron won't disturb you—out of indifference, not kindness. Entrees: $6-$10.

The Palace (1200 Ocean Dr, 531-9077). Where everyone goes after the beach. Salads, pastas, and burgers; best for lunch or afternoon snacking. Service can be abominable—patrons are treated like they've crashed a party. Waiters sigh a lot, don't make eye contact, take your order by coming up to the table and waiting for you speak first, and spend a lot of time talking among themselves. At least they're nice to their friends, who visit often. Entrees: everything under $10.

World Café (719 Lincoln Rd, 534-9095). Offers a small but tempting menu of Thai specialties for lunch or dinner. You dine in an environment created to introduce guests to the cultures of Asia and Africa—this is also a store selling furniture, art, clothes, jewelry, and gifts from India, Africa, and Asia. Entrees: $6-$7.

PLAY/MEET

MOSTLY FOR DANCING

Amnesia (136 Collins Ave, 531-5535). Seasonal dance club open from Oct to late May. Closed Mon. Mixed straight/gay all week; hugely popular tea dance Sun pm.

Diamante (1771 West Ave, 538-5567). The place of the moment on Sat (the only gay night). Six bars and 25,000 square feet on two floors with catwalk, VIP room, x-rated video room. Exotic dancers.

Kremlin (727 Lincoln Rd, 673-3150). Gay-owned and operated. Small, attractive dance club, fall-of-Pompeii Greco-Roman decor. Dance area, couch room for relaxing, and a pool table room. Currently popular on Tue and Thu nights, but call ahead.

Icon (1235 Washington Ave). Super high-tech. Where the old Paragon used to be. Gay only on Fri, when it's the place to be. Glam Slam (very het) other nights.

Paragon (245 22nd St, 534-1235). SoBe's only after-hours bar doesn't get started until real late. 24 hour liquor license. Kind of a dive—nothing like the old Paragon.

153

Warsaw (1450 Collins Ave, 531-4555). As new clubs come on line, old favorites find they must cater to a mixed gay/straight crowd. Such has been the fate of this disco where Sun nights are the hottest (Wed and Fri popular, too).

MOSTLY FOR DRINKING/CRUISING

Boy Bar (821 Lincoln Rd, 534-0887). Chic cocktail bar (formerly Snap). Cabaret/women's night on Thu.

Metro Underground (925 Washington Ave, 538-7883). Relatively new bar, (formerly Hombre) for Levis/leather crowd. Mon is women's night.

Twist (1057 Washington Ave, 538-9478). Of the watering holes, this dark, small, smoky, but attractive place on two levels attracts the youngest, hippest, and cruisiest crowd.

West End Bar (942 Lincoln Rd, 538-9378). Neighborhood place with high ceilings and picture windows where patrons glide in on their Rollerblades for a quick one. Although it's a friendly bar, I watched this gorgeous man standing against a column for several hours, staring vacantly ahead as he nursed his Miller Lite, muscles bulging from his skimpy attire (the top was probably bought at Cabana Joe—see under **Shop**). Hurry—he may still be there.

SHOP

Cabana Joe (12th Street at Ocean Dr, 532-4510). Huge selection of custom-made swim and workout wear (only the fit need apply).

Don't Panic (1249 Washington Ave, 531-7223). Purveyor of witty gay-themed T-shirts and gifts.

GW (720 Lincoln Rd, 534-4763). Sells all manner of sexual paraphernalia, magazines, 4,000 books, cards, and risqué gifts.

Whittal & Schon (1319 Washington Ave, 538-2606). Stocks scores of funky hats (perfect for special parties) and every type of underwear Calvin Klein makes.

RESOURCES

GENERAL INFORMATION

154

Miami Beach Chamber of Commerce (1920 Meridian Ave, 672-1270). Good source for free information.

Miami Design Preservation League's Art Deco Welcome Center (1244 Ocean Drive; 672-2014). Provides information on historic buildings and conducts walking tours.

GAY INFORMATION

SoBe Place Productions (538-3328). Concierge service to give you the latest poop.

South Beach Business Guild (672-9100). The gay chamber of commerce.

BOOKSTORE

GW (720 Lincoln Rd, 534-4763). There is no all-gay bookstore as of this writing, but this shop offers a carefully-chosen selection of gay magazines and books.

Books & Books Inc. (933 Lincoln Rd, 532-3222). Interesting gay section.

PUBLICATIONS

Hotspots (5100 N.E. 12th Ave, Fort Lauderdale 33334, 928-1862). Gay club mag covering all of Florida.

Wire (1638 Euclid Ave, 538-3111). Intelligent weekly of local politics and events.

#

A

B

C

D

E

H

I

J

M

N

163

O

P

Q

R

165

S

T

U

V

W

XYZ

Newcomer's Handbooks™

The original, always updated, absolutely invaluable
guides for people *moving* to a city!

Find out about neigborhoods, apartment hunting, money matters,
deposits/leases, getting settled, helpful services, shopping for the home,
places of worship, belonging, sports/recreation, vounteering, green space,
transportation, temporary lodgings and useful telephone numbers!

	#/COPIES		TOTAL
NEWCOMER'S Atlanta	_____	x $13.95	$_____
NEWCOMER'S Boston	_____	x $13.95	$_____
NEWCOMER'S Chicago	_____	x $12.95	$_____
NEWCOMER'S Los Angeles	_____	x $12.95	$_____
NEWCOMER'S New York City	_____	x $15.95	$_____
NEWCOMER'S Washington, DC	_____	x $13.95	$_____
		SUBTOTAL	$_____
TAX (IL residents add 8.75% sales tax)			$_____
POSTAGE & HANDLING ($4.00 first book, $.75 each add'l)			$_____
		TOTAL	$_____

SHIP TO:

_____
Name

_____
Title

_____
Company

_____
Address

_____   _____   _____
City   State   Zip

_____
Phone Number

Send this order form and a check or money order
payable to: First Books, Inc.

First Books, Inc., Mail Order Department
P.O. Box 578147, Chicago, IL 60657
312-276-5911

Allow 2-3 weeks for delivery.